If you want to create a miracle, see clearly what is in front of you and believe that the desires of your heart manifested it for you.

It often takes time to manifest

Your dreams or to change them.

Perhaps they have already arrived in

A different form or magnitude.

In 2020, I celebrated 200 years of

Pioneering on the same land in three families.

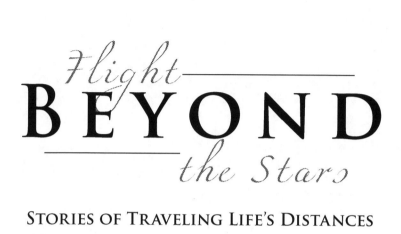

Flight BEYOND the Stars

STORIES OF TRAVELING LIFE'S DISTANCES TOWARD WHOLENESS AND CREATIVITY

JACQUELINE K. KELSEY

2013

authorHOUSE®

A 2021 RE-EDIT
BY BLACK TWIG PRODUCTIONS
at APPLE SHED STORY TELLING CENTER
www.jacquelinekelsey70.com

AuthorHouse™
1663 Liberty Drive
Bloomington, IN 47403
www.authorhouse.com
Phone: 833-262-8899

The stories reflecting the author's journey to wholeness should not be adapted and used by the reader to heal dependencies or physical or emotional illnesses requiring professional treatment. The author does not take responsibility for the reader's use of her experiences.

Published by AuthorHouse 06/11/2021

ISBN: 978-1-4817-5326-5 (sc)
ISBN: 978-1-4817-5327-2 (hc)
ISBN: 978-1-4817-5328-9 (e)

Library of Congress Control Number: 2013908824

Print information available on the last page.

Any people depicted in stock imagery provided by Thinkstock are models, and such images are being used for illustrative purposes only. Certain stock imagery © Thinkstock.

This book is printed on acid-free paper.

Because of the dynamic nature of the Internet, any web addresses or links contained in this book may have changed since publication and may no longer be valid. The views expressed in this work are solely those of the author and do not necessarily reflect the views of the publisher, and the publisher hereby disclaims any responsibility for them.

IN APPRECIATION

Thank you to all of my life teachers—generations of family, professionals, friends from the past and formidable foes. Much affection and devotion has come to me from pets and places. For the production of this book, I appreciate Hans Dietz's informal reactions and suggestions on-going; also edits and understanding of my purpose in a context of philosophy. Janet Gum has persevered in manuscript preparation with unusual carefulness and dependable decisions.

Erin O'Toole's clear directions for complicated text and picture design edits facilitated final galley revisions so that the book designers could easily incorporate my wishes. Adalee Cooney, Assistant Manager of Production, consistently supported the goals of my book design so that I was pleased with the end product as I had envisioned it. Both hometown public and college library staff members helped me with use of computers, essential after editors were finished.

I am grateful for the inner strength from God's grace through life's transitions and the protection He gives me while I continue to spiral toward fulfilling my life's purposes.

A THEMATIC TABLE OF CONTENTS

BASED ON INTRODUCTIONS AND
CONCLUSIONS TO THE CHAPTERS

DEDICATION

When my mother lived out the last few months of her life, I left home to get a short break from caregiving. I had been so close to her that I thought if I did not write my own story I would die. In a week I pulled together thirty pages of narrative and excerpted stories from *Dancing Up the Mountain*, an earlier group of writings on my life and some stories from my trips to Hawaii, Australia, and New Zealand.

During the next year after my mother's passing at age ninety-six, I completed the book.

My mother thought I should live like a "child of the wind" like I was in life transition during six years previously. I had sent her a poem entitled *Butterflies*, which we appreciated together and loved.

GOING AND RETURNING HOME
by
Kathryn Andrews Kelsey

My Mother's Recollection of College Days

"It was on the hikes and picnics that I spent hours dreaming of the future. On these occasions I dreamed of an idyllic day to come when I would travel great distances, see fabulous mountains, rivers and oceans, and feel the thrill of great cities–the world. Little did I know that world was [here]…."

PREFACE

The Flyer

Excerpted from *Dancing up the Mountain,*
A Guide to Writing Your Life Story,
Jacqueline K. Kelsey, PhD,1999

Jacqueline Cochran was a famous aviatrix in the early 1940's. Mother admired her and liked the name. She has always told me that she named me after her. My middle name is Kathryn, after my mother, great grandmother, and great great grandmother. I think it sounds like Cochran. I must connect to women flyers because in the fourth grade I gave a reading for WCTU (Women's Christian Temperance Union) on the life of Amelia Earhart.

"THE EAGLE"

This card was sent to my mother by a childhood chum.

Currently Reeve Lindbergh's children's books top my reading list. I see myself as a flyer in midlife and write life stories about myself in flight. The hawk and the eagle are important birds to me and my children's stories feature birds.

Mother told my naming story along with my late sister's, who was named Stephanie, after a role in the movie *Roberta*.

Cinderella of the Air

Excerpted from *Dancing up the Mountain*
A Guide to Writing Your Life Story,
Jacqueline K. Kelsey, PhD,1999

In my late 60's I investigated, for the second time, the life of Jacqueline Cochran, my name's sake. The first time I had read her biography in a dictionary of famous people at the St. Johnsbury *Athenaeum*. I was surprised to learn about her successful cosmetic business and her record in breaking the sound barrier. My general inquiry fostered my age-related interests. Also, I lived a few miles from Reeve Lindberg, daughter of the famous aviator, Charles Lindberg. Reeve was active in the book community in St. Johnsbury and I had read her life story *Under a Wing*.

Fifteen years later while teaching in Vermont, I read Jacqueline Cochran's autobiography and continued the serendipity of my life connection to her. Her "Cinderella of the Air" appellation suggests the charmed life, the magic of adventure, and the rags to riches sojourn she lived out. In chapter II "Backwards and Forwards" I suggest the same charmed sojourn in the marvelous twenty-four hour Honolulu flight of magic when I too, lived out the Cinderella story, a symbol for my "backward and forward" life. I received the appellation for my flight as a testimony from my Japanese witness. The serendipitous connection with my namesake continued.

Jacqueline Kelsey

A PERSONAL MYTHOLOGY

"While I lay on the massage table in the salon, she whispered over me, 'I was born and grew up in Japan. Are you a stewardess?' She would answer for herself—'No.' She had asked me a series of questions about who I am. 'You are a leader. A teacher—Yes!' She exclaimed, 'We are sisters. You take care of people in the air and I take care of people on the ground.' I began to tell her my story. She said it was the *Cinderella* story."

from *"Sometimes You Have to See the Ocean"*

CHAPTER I

Stovepipe

"... the idea of Spirit traveling through little hollow bones of the Native American woman appealed to me more than the empty, hollow stovepipe through my center."

Coming into Harbor

CHAPTER I

Stovepipe

Our Family Always Had Danced for Fun

When we lived in a Midwest bungalow of our university town, we created a home from my FHA tiny three-bedroom. The small family room served us as a library with books on the north wall, floor to ceiling. The Franklin wood stove stood between two windows on the west across from the back door. My father and Hans labored to get the pipe on so it would fit snugly to the ceiling and look as if it were really going to funnel smoke. Hans gave up leaving my dismayed father to finish the job because Hans did not really care about the stovepipe or the stove. Eventually, at a garage sale I found electric logs that glowed and I set them on top of an electric heater that just fit the stove opening. The room was cozy and we spent holidays and evenings reading by the fire.

After my doctoral program I landed a job across the United States in a start-up graduate program for teacher education. The night before I left, a teacher friend and I dulled our senses in the living room until there was no more to say or think. I could not imagine having to travel to the far West to take a job which I did not really want. Nonetheless, I rented out the house and left my cozy fireside to perch in a lakeside apartment. Although there was no stove, the window view of the lake and tall pines, herons and eagles helped me to soar over time. On clear mornings I could brush by the flaming fuchsia rhododendrons on the stone path to the water's edge to see Mt. Rainier when "she was out."

Ordinarily, nature would be a quick start for my soul. The local paper carried a feature about the point where I lived. According to Native American tradition, the water crossing at the cove was considered a place for the soul's crossing from one life to another. The first year I was dead to any tradition. I was fortunate to get myself through the suburbs. Over time, the bird box on a post at the edge of the neighbor's yard beaconed a symbol of hope. Each morning, a Blue Heron perched in the early morning sun and seemed to wait for my recognition. Because of its reliability I called him the Holy Spirit.

I craved connection because I was alone in suburbia. There were no familiar mid-western touchstones and no people known by me or others from back home. The conservative church which affiliated with my college alma mater did not offer parallel experiences to my personal life or job. Because I wanted new experiences, I explored different denominations. I finally chose one which appealed to my views of what I thought an enlightened Christian view should espouse. I had been churched in evangelicalism and had taught in a Bible college; therefore, I knew the basics and more. In a more holistic approach, from foot washing to Musical Church services, get-a-ways to mountain lodges and church suppers for singles, I began to find camaraderie.

In spite of the philosophical congruity and the social

connectedness, I became aware of my emptiness, a lack of feeling. Our evening musical church had been invited to the home of a couple who had succeeded in business and the arts. My theatre and dance background and current lessons in voice drew me to these people. We played an interactive game, demanding personal responses; I was shocked when it became clear that there was nothing inside of me. I spoke out to the group to describe how I felt using the familiar metaphor of the stovepipe—all form and no real function, like my pretend fireplace in the library back home.

About this time I was reading a book on Native American spirituality, written by a Lutheran minister. He referred to his belief that Spirit traveled through the little hollow bones of the small Native American woman who was aware of herself as a conduit. Because I was seeking spiritual growth, *the idea of Spirit traveling through little hollow bones of the Native American woman appealed to me more than the empty, hollow stovepipe through my center.*

Being a researcher by trade, finding literature on bones intrigued me. Collecting enough references reassured me I was on the right track of body parts to renew myself. Always a dancer, moving my limbs appealed to me. From tap and ballet to the acrobatic role as an Indian princess in grade school, I moved through the decades dancing my way into creative expression.

Our family always had danced for fun at holiday gatherings in the living room and I had studied modern dance in college. My mother sent me a feature article on a Native American ballerina, when I moved to the Northwest,

I pursued dance in a morning modern dance class only to be disappointed because the instruction was strictly formatted like lessons for ballroom dance steps which I turned away from after two sessions. Finally, the instructor allowed me free rein when I persuaded him to let me follow him intuitively. Of course, I soared because I am a natural dancer. What was unnatural would follow.

There was a lack of emotional connection with the modern dance teacher. Perhaps I wanted too much because I was attracted to him. But with my hollow stovepipe mentality I could not tell whether or not I caused the problem. The lack of intimacy affected my spontaneity. There could be no synchronicity between us.

The Dervish

When the teacher danced with me I felt that he was in St. Elsewhere. During my harangue, "Where were you?" he replied that the room was filled with spirits and that he had been dancing with them.

The next week I sat cross-legged on the wooden floor and confronted him about the previous week and the strange image being on top of his face. It was another layer of another face not solid but like an energy source. It looked like him but was not. The false smile was exaggerated and the eyes were slits.

"Who are you?" I asked. "I think you know," he replied. "You little dervish; get away from me," I screeched and shot up from the floor. I never returned.

ॐ

Would the stovepipe become a conduit like little hollow bones? Would I express spirit? How? The mystery had revealed itself; my spiritual nature could read reality. My entire body was a sensor not just my bones and I could see with spiritual discernment after all.

At this time, I could not feel much but emotional pain. I would weep my way through Musical Church and the minister would sidle down the aisle near me and pat my shoulder. I am sure he wondered if I would ever come around. Believe it. The day church let me give workshops. I was so spiritually effective that I stopped leading the group because I could tell the quick results for the most difficult personalities and I did not know where I would lead them. I did not trust myself and certainly not them. I suppose I was farther out spiritually from what I realized. Years of growth had prepared me unawares even though I could not feel, recall or appreciate. In total, I was impacting others.

Even though I doubted my own capacities, I volunteered to head up a program for church services in area nursing homes. Our program grew to five homes and forty volunteers. Each Sunday we met at all five resident homes and sang songs, read Scripture, poetry, quips, comics—whatever would keep interest. We cared deeply. The range of folks' abilities spanned from Alzheimer's disease to mild dementia. Over the months, I created stories, recorded them and developed programming for staff and families at the facilities. One of my favorite stories shows how humble people were to be sources of healing for me.

A Face

Excerpted from *Listen in the Moment*
to Timeless Folks, C.D.
Jacqueline K. Kelsey, PhD, 2003

On a Saturday afternoon I visited the Alzheimer's unit to deliver meditation booklets to the residents. I went upstairs and got off the elevator. Across the room there was a table of ladies sitting, playing games. One of the women I knew very well. I walked up to the table and greeted Beverly. She was in her own world, gazing into space, twisting her hair.

As soon as I came into her view, she started. She stopped twisting her hair and smiled at me. When I handed her the meditation booklet, she took it gratefully. "I hope that you enjoy reading the meditation this week, I encouraged." She looked at me with a soft focus and said, "What I will enjoy, what I will remember is your face each time I see these pages; and then she said, "I love you." I hugged her and told her that I loved her, too. When I turned away from the table to greet others, I heard her say again, "I love you" and yet a third time I heard, "I love you."

A story about men in the city who visit maternity wards late at night illustrates, the same love. Dressed in business suits, after a long hard day they visited the newborn wards. The men would hold and rock the babies, lying alone for hours with no one to hold them. The giving between the men and babies shows that babies not only need to receive but to give their love. By those men being there, those babies were allowed to give love. And the men received it.

Similarly with Beverly, my being there allowed Beverly to give her love. I heard a voice and the voice affirmed for me that I was loveable. The next time I visited we greeted and she looked into my face with detachment and spoke a candid observation, "You have a nice face." Even though she did not seem to remember me the next time I visited, I will know that Beverly is a person who is able to give and to receive love.

⅋

I was challenged during this time. The greatest test was finding my car after work in the mall. I would wander the underground parking lot too long because I did not keep track. Of course, I improved. Still two years later I could not compute fast in a linear way. On the job, I was unable to do simple tasks like linear inventory. My employer would return at the end of the afternoon to find me still checking in a large order.

Also, there was a long-term basic deficit. I was never good at linear work or mechanical tasks, like punching a switchboard. I left the company because I was overwhelmed by being a receptionist, using four lines. Put me on the floor selling perfumes or art objects and I would excel. My selling skills were persuasive because of looks and character, good taste and caring for people. I always made employers money. Some of my knack was genetic. My father and grandfathers were good salesmen. However, for what I got paid, I could hardly exist on the money.

A seemingly appropriate university job I had to leave because it was unsuitable for my philosophy and training. I came from a leading teacher education school in the country. I was a round peg in a square hole. I had turned down a university job in the Midwest because I knew full well how to anticipate the difficulty of teaching between two departments. The money was not great for the long haul and promotion would have been slow and grueling. Microcosm and macrocosm misplacement showed up in my artistic world and larger intellectual life.

A spiritual quest led me to stay put. My life would be unstructured, unpredictable, and creative without any hint of financial provision. Choices and circumstances left me in harm's way, it appeared, except for intermittent jobs and rent money from my house in the Midwest. The stovepipe was filling with life choices based on who I really was becoming—an artist.

Art in Common Life

Over the holidays I worked at a major department store selling perfume. It was a good job for me—four hours a day, being with people, a beautiful environment. Selling came easy for me and they liked to have me. "Roma," an Italian designer perfume, was my favorite fragrance. The final Christmas that I sold perfume, I was offered a line selling Gucci. 'Lo and Behold' the name and marketing matched my doctoral research topic—"art in common life."

During the postdoctoral fun years I "learned by experience." My mother observed I was living a lifestyle I had written about for the previous six years.

ॐ

Every promising workshop idea or small job was praised by my coffee group and promoted by them. "She is coming out of her slump—she is doing…." One of my practical friends had made it by developing a cleaning business and was willing to train me. I, too, had been practical when I was a teenager and in college.

Even after my MA and four years of college teaching, I continued to wait tables to get me to the next step. The "strawberry pie job" helped us move to my husband's PhD studies in the Midwest when he roofed as a trade-off for my stint. I started off as the coffee counter waitress with no tips. At the end of the shift, I scooped out old pie shells and refilled them with slick viscous jell even if the berries shadowed mold. In college I had worked at an all-night truck stop to earn money to go to Mexico with my Spanish teacher. Surely, hands-on work would lead me forward again as it did in college and during early years of career building. Life experience put me in "good stead," as my father would say.

I Saw the World the Other Night

When I was a junior in college, my Spanish teacher and her assistant from Mexico City packed me and a friend, along with her children, into their family car. The primitive travel to the border and crowded stay in the Mexican family's home was all worth the high view from the tower in Mexico City.

For the first time I was in a new culture, another country. Home seemed far away. When I looked over the city at night, life seemed to dance and hold promise. I felt I had seen the world. I was reminded of the opening line in a 17th century metaphysical poem by Henry Vaughan: "I saw eternity the other night, Like a ring of pure and endless light; All calm as it was bright, and round beneath it, Time in hours, days, and years. Driv'n by the spheres like a vast shadow mov'd; in which the world and all her train were hurl'd…"

There seemed to be no lights in the cleaning jobs. I was in mid-life and I could not see that cleaning would lead to any higher goal even though twenty dollars an hour for cleaning was good money. The jobs passed on to me from my friend were ones she had finished with. I learned that I would be seen as "the cleaning girl" and treated with the disrespect of someone who cleaned up after others even when there was not much to clean up, or, most disgustingly when the same mess re-appeared each week as a ritual to justify the need for my job. Bathtubs were the most offensive places to clean. Leaning over the bent wand of a vacuum cleaner to sweep a tidy white carpet or leaving no streaks on a marble kitchen counter perfectly smooth at start led to despair over form and function. I simply walked away. The price for survival income was too great and could not tie me over until I reached a higher place.

The stint of summer school teaching proved to be as bad. I was an alternative teacher who helped failing kids in English to make up the year's credit. Many "wiseacres" who were plain lazy—had the skills but had not applied themselves—resolved to show off and disrupt the class to prove to the principal that I was not meeting their needs. The principal sided with them, of course, and my former years of successful alternative teaching for non-college bound students seemed like a far-away dream. How could a successful teacher be failing so miserably? Not fitting the temperament, the atmosphere, or the role, I could not stand up for myself. I was under-employed. Returning to work I had left in order to get a PhD to teach at the university level, I could not engender enough self-respect to tell them where to get off. I felt like my cat with kidney disease. He had eaten low protein foods for so long that he had no muscle mass. He just doubled over when I held him.

By substitute teaching in five districts, rural and suburban, I tried to "up the ante" with success especially in the rural area, like my hometown in the Midwest. A long-term subbing job in the suburbs came up but the demand was rigorous. Was I headed for numbing again to create life through an empty stovepipe because of life's failures as they seemed to me?

Morning Field Walk

No lights up the hill to my apartment so I walked in the dark to the bottom to catch an early morning bus to a nearby suburb. I had to switch at the bus depot and take a bus to the outer regions of the city limits where I was dropped off to walk a mile in the dark across a field to get to the school by 7:30 a.m. It must have taken an hour.

This was a possible six-week subbing stint in special education with elementary children. Having been a regular classroom teacher for fourteen years, I entered the situation with authority and stature. However, I was viewed as too much of an authoritarian. I was an experienced teacher in a substitute's role. The job did not last long because of the supervisor's discouraging attitude toward me and my style.

ℬℭ

A Pipe Dream

I had done a lot of dirty work in my life and never shied away. I felt lucky to have any job but I was sweeping up the wrong floors. In recent years I had heard a TV woman evangelist, aspiring to be a leader, tell how she was instructed by an elder to be willing to sweep floors. She repeatedly swung her cute hips and a make-believe broom. I had already gone through the paces thirty years earlier starting at the bottom, humbly sweeping floors. Now I was starting all over after I had prepared for eight years to re-start at a higher level. How many times would I start over and work up only to be at the bottom?

In looking back I see that I had given up making money in creative ways. Because it did not work regardless of how successful I had been in tutoring, creating workshops, and teaching in adult community education and park districts. It was time for a change, time to admit I was helpless, and live like a child of the wind. My own efforts were bankrupt in ideas on how to earn money. Although all of my workshops succeeded, regular teaching posts had not worked. As an alternative teacher, invariably I chose conservative environments which did not promote my teaching goals or style. As a result, I was always swimming upstream. Where was the right place?

When I tried college/university teaching, even though I succeeded in my goals and could show tremendous learning results in my students, I was challenged by competing teachers in the department. If a heavy-handed chairperson became authoritative I found it difficult to stand up for myself.

On one job, I was not fired but my access to the department secretary was cut off and my office space, too; perhaps it was due to financial cutbacks. My reason for not doing well was articulated by the chair correctly—"a round peg in a square hole." I tried to fit a holistic teaching philosophy into a curriculum with linear learning and objective evaluations.

A hollow stovepipe seemed to be an appropriate symbol for not only my inability to have feelings but for my choice of right-life work and place. What would be the pay-off professionally for my emotional healing? How would they dovetail? I would start over. I would give up everything to get there—the right self-expression.

In artistic expression I could bring my total self to bear, but in the process, how could I take care of myself?

My reason for coming west was due to ending a job for which the department wanted seemingly to hire a "hard researcher" to build the department's reputation. Instead, i was a theoretical researcher who had created a worldview based on inter-disciplinary nature resources, to use as a philosophical contexts for teaching cultural folklore in rural schools. The study was illustrative rather than being a proof study. I was a one-year teacher. Because I would have left anyway, after the second year, I did not mind leaving had I known earlier and been able to find another job. I was left "holding the bag" at a late date.

Not wanting to nor able to fit into traditional university teaching, nor desiring substitute teaching roles on going, and unskillful in hands-on work, I was asking how I could earn a living. What could I do to take care of myself? Perhaps more important to me, I asked, "Who would I become? Been there, done that!!!! I am middle aged.

CHAPTER II

Backward and Forward

"Low in the sky a plane hummed softly toward me. With resolution the words spoke themselves. 'The war is over.' I was transgressing time—back to World War II."

from *Sometimes You Have to See the Ocean*

My brother, sister, and I at the edge of Lake Michigan

CHAPTER II

Backward and Forward

Dreams to be Dreamed

Recently at the nursing home, a resident seated in the hallway stopped me for conversation with his "starter" about the shape of the world and the openness of time. He finished with the suggestion that I ponder "backward and forward" at the same time and said he thought I should write a story on the idea. Indeed, I had returned to the same places to get a jumpstart because I was comfortable and familiar with my former journey.

In the interim my life did progress and in this chapter I show how going backward led me forward. On the fifteenth year after leaving the green-gold turf of the northwest, I returned to it to celebrate my life going forward. I boarded the bus to downtown just for the ride by familiar places—the third-story dance studio where I took ballroom dance, the warehouse which housed a film-making studio above the oriental rug company, the place of many scenes for me, and the commercial building where I taught a well-received evening adult class in life-story writing. The following story is part of the backwards view which I see took me forward.

Like when I was a teen-ager moving out, my mid-life required the same rebellion to find my identity when I left the Midwest and the stereotypes of traditional expectations. During my teen-age years, there was no experience to prepare me for a serene role which I desired. Rather I was typecast as the Natalie Wood character, with James Dean in *Rebel without a Cause*. I preferred the character, however, rather than sedate middle-aged roles I was typecast for later because of my middle-age looks. I retained the rebellion past middle age.

Backwards and forward were familiar issues. What would be the role I was in? How would I take the part and join it with the present? Where would I go?

"Sometimes You Have to See the Ocean" contains the "Cinderella" theme of being someone else but disguised and the reasons for it. The way out is dramatized in real life at the Magic Show in its story by the airplane I see while walking peacefully along the ocean afterwards. Seeing a photo of the opposite of who I was confirmed me to be a beautiful dancer like the Hawaiian girl who acknowledged me after the show when she came off stage to my table and hugged me.

Rebel without a Cause

In my senior year in high school I acted the lead role in the play version of the movie starring James Dean and Natalie Wood.

During the scene when the daughter and father are arguing, he slapped me in the face instead of faking a slap. I did not let it phase me but the audience was shocked and sounds came forth. I do not remember how the director handled it. I do not remember an apology from the actor/father.

℞

Similar to the cover-up of feelings on stage, when I taught high school English I always smiled and my principal rewarded me by telling me how much he liked that feature about me. Because the job was so stressful and I did not have the inner stuffing to weather it; I could not "walk away" at the end of the day. I ran to a counselor weekly. One of the first behaviors he wanted me to get rid of was smiling all the time as if my world were okay. It was hard to learn how to act. Expressing feelings was not part of my family's way and certainly not of my husband's. Is it any wonder that my doctoral dissertation advisor observed that there was no feeling in my writing? It was all cerebral, written from an almost machine mind. My stovepipe had been in place.

As I think back to high school days, it is a bit like being cast for the nurse's role in *Romeo and Juliet* rather than in the beautiful Juliet's role. What was there about me to be cast in the nurse's role? I was a character myself! Last fall on Broadway, what delight I felt when Mary Poppins, carried by her umbrella, wafted above the theatre audience. There are dreams to be dreamed and lived out.

I wonder if there is a role I would like to play? Probably not, because I enjoy myself so much and believe I do more good in bringing my belief message to people day by day and directly by my life. But if I could be an influence and the character were to be type-cast, I would want to fly like Mary Poppins. The message about life would be that it is metaphysical and that the idealism of the far away and primitive is part of the romance. The role I created is Cinderella in "Sometimes You Have to See the Ocean." I have flown forward into a new rebel role—of Cinderella.

The Accident

I can see in retrospect how fearless I learned to become traveling at night by myself in the city, driving, taking the bus, and walking.

One night coming from my film class I drove by a scene where police had pulled up in front of a bar. It looked as if someone were lying on the sidewalk.

I had the sense that something awful had happened. It took me a long time to get over it. Probably I connected it with seeing other ugly scenes either in childhood or "another life" or in movies. The reality was too close.

∛

How relaxing to be riding and reviewing, to see all of the "backwards" from a new place. After several hours, my experience had aggregated and focused in its purest form of showing the successes. I could see and feel my heart's aspirations and successful expressions in the arts—recording, acting, dancing, singing, and writing. My six years lifted me beyond my expectations.

In the midst of the "bankruptcy" when I could feel only losses and struggles, the mountains behind the lake had raised me. I had always been able to see the spiny topped range poking up behind the orange cranes and cargo ships. Off the bus, once again the ferry whirred to get me and other commuters to the island across the bay; squawking gulls syncopated the flipping waves against the boat. I would breathe easy over a latte with the locals at the dock café on the other side.

On the revisit Saturday near the sailboat docks, my former hometown celebrated a healthy-living day. In the park area musicians sang. Tables, samples, displays, and gifts invited clean living. One table displayed body parts in solution and also lain out on the tables for passersby to pick up and examine. I was aghast when the interpreter told the life story about the person whose liver one could hold. The approach reminded me of stories heard fifteen years ago to help people move toward healthy choices. At the present time my work life expressed creativity in writing and recording in the East, caretaking of my parents and their farm in the Midwest, and traveling the world beyond—Hawaii to the South Pacific. At one table of presenters, I talked to a writer who shared her beleaguering experience of publishing her story. I had thought about writing my sojourn in life but was not encouraged by her testimony.

After I moved to the East and Midwest, I returned almost yearly to the healing vortex of the Northwest's waters and mountains. I was still suckling to get the last bit of goodness to last me forever. On going, I made a triangle from the Northwest to Hawaii from Hawaii to the Midwest and East. The whirligig rotation of places could have been pinned to a toy stick for just the joy of movement in the wind. However, the stories I lived and told from each adventure were surely intertwined on levels I could not imagine because they never would have happened without each other.

For example, before a return trip to the Midwest I received a message during an informal conversation with my neighbor who lives weekends on an East coast island: "Sometimes you have to see the ocean." The idea flung me to Hawaii for twenty-four hours with only $200. When my neighbor friends moved back to their island home, nature created a monument in front of her house on the river bank. A five-inch, round log lay on the ground underneath a V-shaped branch which had blown, with force, into the top of the base log. The freestanding monument withstood the rains and the wind. Of course, I mentally took its picture and it imprinted my mind with the message of man's oneness with nature and the contiguity in all places.

Last week I gave a workshop to an Alzheimer's support group

in a local hospital near our farm town in the Midwest. Similarly, I had done this in the East several years ago when I tried to recreate life work which I had done in the Northwest. This time I enacted the stories with a deliberate intention to be more expressive with my interpretive skills. It was a small gesture but seemed to cause me to gather myself in a big way. The life story emphasis was to help people hold on to and build their memories. I was familiar with their loss. The entire fall I had been creating opportunities to tell stories, to present myself, rather than to read or play a CD.

Recently a psychic out East told me that I am dealing with an issue of submission to domination by family which comes out of old stuff—having land taken away from me in a past life. Yesterday, I drove to ancestral moorings in New Hampshire. En route from Vermont I recalled more specifically how the daughter in the family had land given to her to preserve. Driving to the village, picturing the rows of family houses on the ridge hill below Rice Mountain, "I let go and let God in" and hopefully healed myself a bit.

In New Hampshire, at the Lenten soup supper two weeks ago our minister asked, "Where do you need healing?" Sunday I plan to meet with another congregational minister to help me with the problem of domination. Maybe I can go backwards to my sixth generation New Hampshire ancestors and heal their domination.

My heritage and love of the mountains connect me to New Hampshire. I located my fifth great grandmother's 200-year-old handwritten marriage record in the town clerk's office in Alsted.

Fast forwarding, an image of Singapore and the natural beauty of Bora Bora came up this week. How will I get there and when? And whatever for? I do not usually ask the question; I just go. I have air miles from my Australian/New Zealand trip. I am going out farther and farther and farther. Do I think that time and patience will catapult me? No, it is my courage like taking my trip to Australia and New Zealand.

Jean Batten, Queen of the Air

Three times until success—first flight from New Zealand to England. They prepared a runway for her where the international airport is now. She used maps and a compass only and landed between flags. Six thousand people gathered and car lights provided the light to make the runway visible.

Am I a Queen of the Air? What will I aspire to and achieve?

ॐ

As we had neared the airport to come to the East, I stopped and soared with awe as the plane jettisoned off the runway. I could feel the energy of its rise and the grace of a lift. Having arrived at our woodsy home along the river I absorbed myself in the embers of the woodstove fire. I settled down to life in the Northwoods, noticing the mantle display of bisque eagles, gifts from Mother. Ordinarily, I like more refined art objects but we lived in the woods at the bottom of the mountain along the river. With nostalgia, I recalled the owlet on our farm let loose, as an adult, to its freedom; we held a night ceremony near the house and field, with the woods in view.

Memory of the eagles on the mantel melded with memory of four eagles flying by my second-story apartment perch over the lake in the Northwest woods. I am bent on independence now and these triumphant birds show me what is new, although they have been present in my life all along as harbingers of my own creative soaring. Having finished taking care of my mother to take care of myself, I am no longer dependent on a partner to take care of me. Part of domination is servitude which now leaves me of necessity.

Sometimes You Have to See the Ocean—
This is Your Japan Day
Part I

While I lay on the massage table in the salon, she whispered over me, 'I was born and grew up in Japan. Are you a stewardess?' She would answer for herself—'No.' She had asked me a series of questions about who I am. 'You are a leader. A teacher—Yes!' She exclaimed, 'We are sisters. You take care of people in the air and I take care of people on the ground.' I began to tell her my story. She said it was the Cinderella *story.*

I had begun the day with a Japan Air tote attached to my suitcase. The Japanese lady from housekeeping at the hotel lopped it over the counter. My winter sweater and slacks, neatly folded, jostled in the bag, which said, "Going Far." My load was appreciably lighter now with most of the cold weather clothes, books, snow boots and papers returned to New England. It felt as if I were set for a journey. My plan was still to return to the Midwest.

I had left Maine with twenty dollars, which John had given me and my own two-hundred from my savings for an insurance premium. Before leaving Maine, I had called a counselor in the Northwest area and she confirmed that it sounded like Seattle was as far as I could see myself going. What a leap I already had made to take a week-ender flight, even to get to Seattle. By going all the way to Honolulu I would give up my way back to St. Louis because the week-ender was for a round-trip flight, Chicago to Seattle.

At the O'Hare Airport I approached the gate, unsure whether to bank on using my frequent flyer to Hawaii which would assure me a return to St. Louis from Honolulu. What would I live on when I got there? I could not see my way to go farther or even if I did not, to get home, but I would take the first step and figure out the rest later. The desk flight attendant said I would have to go back to the main terminal to pay for the ticket. That settled it. There was no more time. Yet in a moment of choice, with ten minutes to takeoff, the attendant chose "yes," and I responded to his willingness to put me on the flight to Seattle.

My neighbor had given me the vision when I left New England and when she said, "Sometimes you have to see the ocean." She was speaking of her own need to return to the coast during the time she lived inland. I harbored the cue to take me on.

On the steps of the luxury Waikiki hotel, I overlooked the torch-lit drive and the gardens as I watched for my luggage. By mistake, my luggage had been taken by someone else off the wicky-wicky bus from the airport. Even if I had had my suitcase, it had no Hawaii clothes in it. I had packed my Hawaii bag as part of creating an experience to manifest the trip when I was in New England, but I actually had to leave it at home because my mind would not allow me to decide ahead of time to go, and also, to carry that much extra baggage was impossible, physically. I must have been determined to make it all the way but now I only would have my Japan Air bag stuffed with my red winter sweater and navy slacks and my dirty laundry in my backpack. But still I waited expectantly.

I counted my money. How could I stay at the beach-side hotel? The $300.00 which my partner had wired to me, for which I had waited three extra days in Washington, was almost half gone. Only $180.00 left because I had sent in the rest of the insurance premium I owed for an insurance upgrading due to my new age bracket.

At the hotel desk, I summoned my courage, hoping that my credit card would be approved. As I stood waiting for the paper work to be completed, I received a beautiful, purple orchid lei but soon after was told they could not accept the card in my partner's name. My lei felt defamed. I turned down the offer that was so kindly made to wire John. It was really too late; it was two o'clock in the morning, New England time, and there was no way that he would okay a $250.00 room. Besides, there would be no place from which he could send a fax at this time of night. The desk clerk sent me to the hotel next door for a less expensive room.

I realized I could not spend all my money on the hotel and have no money left for food or an airport shuttle back to the Honolulu Airport. Even so, I walked over to the nearby open-air lobby surrounded by expensive shops and tourist tables set up for the Japanese visitors. I knew the credit card situation would be the same. In good conscience I could not ask. Resolved, I turned back and said to myself, "I will stay at my first choice of hotels." But how?

As I returned to the lobby persevering my way through to find a room, I looked through the arch out to the ocean and saw several people sleeping on mats. Could I do it? I was willing. My suitcase still unreturned, I hung out wandering through the lobby and into the restroom. The attendant confirmed that it was unsafe to sleep on the beach.

When I returned once more to the desk, a young man asked me if he could help me. He said that I could go to my room readily, because it was so late after a long flight and I could fax John in the morning. They would send my luggage up when it came. Instead of accepting immediately, I still wanted to wait for my luggage but more than that I was legalistic about the situation and needed to call John to get approval to make sure that he would approve the amount. What if he would refuse or be terribly angry with me? I told the assistant manager that I would get an exact amount for approval. And he, corresponding to my fear, wanted an approval for all charges itemized. He became nervous when I was more fastidious: "The fax would be due first thing in the morning." He said he would be in his office by nine if I needed to talk with him and he agreed, "This was a most unusual request."

The next morning I awoke to the birds and called John again to see if he had sent the fax approving all itemized expenses on his credit card so that I would not have to ask the assistant manager if all was okay. What a jump for me to move from wanting something to actually asking and receiving it. I actually was trembling when I thought about spending $250.00 on myself for a room for one night. Although I did it with fear and feelings of lack of worth, I had to move quickly in it to receive what I wanted.

I took my time leaning out the balcony window, over the garden setting of the remnant Royal Garden palms. The manager had upgraded my room to garden view. John could hear the birds, too, as we talked on the phone. We agreed this would be the last call during this arduous seven-day trip from New England to the Midwest via Seattle and Hawaii. Every day we had talked once or twice to check in and report that all was okay and to share in how I was making my way. Each step had been precarious, like finding large stones in a raging river rather than stepping stones in a quiet stream.

For twenty-four hours I treated myself to sleep followed by a feast of the most wonderful waking twelve hours of my life—the fullest day of my life. I stayed in my room almost all morning sitting in the sun, listening to the birds, feeling royal under the palms. Throughout the day as I emerged from my room, personnel greeted me at several junctures inquiring how I was and more or less "monitored" my exquisite time. First thing in the morning, I made an appointment with the massage therapist. When she whispered, "We are sisters," I thought of the Japan Air bag and how my expectations had opened to let me hear her speak those words now.

We made an appointment together to finish the massage at the end of the day, before my return flight at 10:00 p.m., because she only had available a half-hour in the morning because of a cancellation. After we had bonded for more good to come between us, I dressed and went upstairs to the outdoor restaurant, located on the beach, almost on the sand.

They were serving a noon buffet. To get the buffet on my room charge I had to eat too fast, so I went back to the desk and asked for an extension beyond one o'clock checkout time, so that I could be leisurely. When I returned to the buffet, I feasted on an array of seafood salads, tropical fruit, and coconut desserts displayed among vibrant red and yellow, lush tropical flowers.

I lay on a chaise lounge under an umbrella for a long while enjoying the warmth of the white sand beach, the clear blue water, and the relaxed feeling of the people around me. Before long, the beach filled with sunbathers and people resting under their umbrellas, reading their books and enjoying cool juices.

It was time for me to check out and I decided to enjoy the hotel service to the fullest. I had asked the desk clerk about using the charge and he said I was able to use it until my plane left at night. At the concierge's desk I tried to schedule the Polynesian Cultural Center trip, but the return to the hotel was too late in the evening for me to catch my flight. Instead I found an ad for a magic show at a nearby hotel. The concierge said that it was a good show, almost equal to the Polynesian. I decided to have dinner at the magic show. Both dinner and show I could put on my room bill as well as my massage when I would return to the hotel before taking a taxi to the airport, my Cinderella coach.

All of my desires were provided for. Every wish that I had was met. Feeling fulfilled and secure with an exciting agenda for the evening, I returned to the beach to relax. I would go swimming, even though I had no suit. Dressed in my navy wool slacks and a navy silk turtleneck, I headed to the pool area where the guys were setting up umbrellas and chairs. I told the fellows I had checked out but wanted to use the guest services for the day.

I buried my billfold in the sand under the little table next to my chaise lounge. Sunglasses and lotion on top of the little table, I began to undress underneath my towel. I folded the top of my turtleneck under to form a straight edge with the shoulder line and I tied the sleeves around my chest. My back was uncovered. I looked like I was wearing a tube-top and it covered me down to the bottom of my panties. I had taken off my wool slacks and rolled them in a package that I put under the chaise lounge. My pink cotton panties looked like a high-cut suit bottom, so I began to walk along the water and I let myself get totally wet. Finally, I was in the ocean. The first time in my four visits to Hawaii.

I remember almost drowning in Lake Michigan when I was three or four. Whatever my prohibition about being in the ocean, now my whole body was symbolic of joining, of being part of life during my swim. Victoriously I walked the white sand beach for a one-half mile past several hotels and resorts and then returned to rest.

Part II

Watching the beautiful bodies, I listened to the hotel band music swaying the people into the water and back again. I was sitting under an umbrella in a chaise lounge, relaxing like other people, no longer an observer, standing on the outside of life. It was time for me to get dressed and to return to the salon for a Jacuzzi before getting ready for the dinner show. On the beach, I decided to dress and it seemed to take as long for discreet dressing as it did undressing. Returning to the beach checkout cabana, I washed the sand off my feet before heading down to the salon. As I walked through the pool gate, past the checkout center for beach chairs, I heard the band from next door playing "Tiny Bubbles."

When I had gone to hear Don Ho the last time I was in Honolulu, he gave us signed cards with our name and his, signed with the word, "Ohana," Family. Before my trip, not knowing I would go to Hawaii, I had sent Don Ho a fax hoping for some kind of connection. The fax was the response in part to his Internet page which I had read in the local library in the middle of winter. He beckoned; "Don Ho gives you your wish from Hawaii." There was nothing else available from the Internet ad. Someone else had won the trip and the song would not play on the sound portion. I wrote to him saying I was spiritually attuned to Hawaii and loved her. Hearing the band play *Tiny Bubbles* struck me with its timeliness.

What a lovely offer for me to be able to use the salon for the day. It almost felt as if I had expanded my room to my own spa. I would be able to shower and relax and get ready for the dinner at the magic show. Through the colonnade corridor, down the carpeted hallway, across the garden through an art gallery on the lower level, I entered the salon.

When I opened the door to the Jacuzzi, I saw a five-foot high mountain of bubbles, the water was running and the bubbles kept growing. Frantically and quietly, I knocked on every door in the massage parlor. I had to tell someone to "turn back the ocean." When a young man came out to help me, he saw the mountain and explained, "I don't know who ordered this up for you." Sheepishly, I gave testimony to the universe, not wanting to think or say *Tiny Bubbles* or Don Ho. Sometime later, I thought of the hotel band playing when I walked through the beach gate to go to the Jacuzzi.

I wondered how my Japanese interest would be carried further on this trip. I hoped I would be with some Japanese people at the magic show and, of course, I was seated with a tourist group of twenty-five Japanese people. There was one seat left next to the only one who spoke English and just as soon as I was seated by the hostess, she came by again and re-seated me at another table, next to an American couple. Upset that I could not continue sitting with the Japanese, I asked the hostess to be moved back; she was not going to let me! I became insistent about the place where I wanted to sit, and so she moved me back.

When I looked around, almost the whole room was filled with Japanese tourists and the girl sitting next to me reminded me that

"Japan is only five hours away." She, too, was a teacher and we had talked about the appeal of my life story workshops at her school. The couple across the table shared their smiles and the printed program for the evening. They graciously nodded hello, many times, when she explained who I was.

What great wonder of disappearing people and energetic fire dancing, an extravaganza sight and sound show. The theme "Magic is seeing and seeing is believing" whirled like a pinwheel inspiring awe, as if there was no ending or beginning. Finally, I could see there was no ending and beginning. Truly seeing is believing; believing is seeing. I wondered about the truth that the magic show was trying to illustrate and my own faith.

At the finale, the whole cast squeezed into a tiny hut on stilts and on command the house disappeared. A fantastic visual as the magician called out, "Building your house on concrete, seeing is not reliable either." The turnabout that confirmed his message was in reality, "faith is the necessary ingredient, because even in the end, seeing is not believing."—A highly entertaining, complex experience to create faith in the audience.

During the show, I had established eye contact and energy with the beautiful hula dancer, the star of the show. The most beautiful woman I had ever seen, in body and spirit. When she came off the stage with the other performers to walk through the audience, she saw that she was near me. She excitedly came over to hug me. It seemed that I was her focus. How wonderful! After the performance, the Japanese girl who I sat next to at dinner sought me out of the crowd and asked me to stand with her parents for a picture. Someone else took the picture of all of us and she took down my address so that she could send me the picture and be in touch with me.

The show was over. Musing and meditatively I walked toward the beach through splendorous tropical gardens joining the hotel with the beach walk. As I circled around the very large planter with the ocean walk in full view, my eye caught the shine of a photo on the ground. When I stooped to pick it up, oh, my heart sank. A pornographic photo. What a contrast with the beautiful imprint of the lovely hula dancer and the picture of my new Japanese friend with me. I thought of the truth I knew that evil brings itself up against the beauty of truth. Ugliness reared its horrible head and also demanded to be seen. Equal time. Looking out toward the ocean, I looked forward to my massage. This trip was not over, even at the end of my walk back to the hotel.

It was a long beach walk. Within fifteen minutes the sky was dark blue. I assured myself that I was safe, alone on the beach for a long walk—what tremendous timing with just the right amount of time to get back and time enough to enjoy the ocean again for an emersion walk to take it all in. I pressed lightly on the sand and feeling complete and fulfilled, I was hardly aware of walking, in my state of all being well. Nothing was missing. The warm air bathed me as the ocean waves had during the afternoon. The tall way I carried myself told me of the intactness that I felt. I needed nothing; totally nurtured, I was able to be fully in touch with the moon and the water and the sand and to feel peace in the world and myself. There was no separation—like a baby must feel in the womb and yet I knew the vast landscape around me.

Low in the sky a plane hummed softly toward me. I stopped to follow its sky path moving over and beyond me. With resolution the words spoke themselves. 'The war is over' I was transgressing time—back to World War II. I had been a war baby. Now I was in the same time and place fifty years after the re-opening of the hotel when it had been used by the American Military for R&R during the war. The war in me was over. We were at peace on my Japan Day. I was free from conflict to fully be myself, to be alone.

My Japan Day had come—An armistice with the past and all that was symbolized for me growing up—the fear of not surviving the war, the prejudice against the Japanese—inexplicable, unidentifiable—the need to be protected, perhaps. The particulars were not important. But the new place that I found myself in by following my leads was indeed life giving. I had been willing to give up my life that I might find it. It came when I saw the ocean. "Sometimes you have to see the ocean" my neighbor had said, "the larger picture—the calm of the ocean and being a part of God. One with myself."

Yesterday, when I had checked into the Waikiki hotel, it was the beginning of the Chinese New Year. The Japanese massage therapist told me this as I received my final massage gift from her. As I left her and the spa and ended my day, I reached into my pocket to show her the desk clerk's card who had made my stay possible, the one who was willing to receive a fax from "Mr. John" in the morning, and who gave me a garden view with birds, whose voices John would share over the phone, as well. Instead of his card, I held my audiocassette tape which I had made on "Listening in the moment." I had brought it with me to give it to him as a thank-you token. Instead, my hand pointed toward her and I willingly gave it up to her and knew that she was the proper recipient. Responding very quickly, heartfelt with gratefulness, she assured me that I would be her source of learning. My words would make her well. She was experiencing great life difficulty and said that her faith in God was great to always bring her more than she needed when she was in need and I had been the client to fill her canceled appointment that morning.

The next afternoon, I arrived in St. Louis, tired from the week's sojourn. This journey was my interlude before beginning a three-week Life Story workshop in my hometown. Praying for the right people and the right number, I had concerns that my not being at home would hold back what should be coming to me. But each time I called the coordinator, I heard two, seven, thirteen, and when I began the workshop, dressed in my island print outfit and Kukui nut lei, the room was circled by twenty-five people. My parents were the last to come in. Looking into the room, they decided that this could not be the place because there were so many unexpected guests. People from eight surrounding farm towns had come and some had brought friends. I believed they were waiting to receive the celebration of their lives as they wrote their stories of journey and magic.

ॐ

Nature's monument

Time and Place are One

See page 23 for commentary on the Triangle of Life.

To Heal and Hold Faith

Seeing "time as one" is possible when viewing both backward and forward in one's life and having the awareness of the same stories re-running behind and in front of each other in linear time with new results; this unity creates balances in life:

- Backward to childhood with its intrusive conflicts through teenage years.
- Forward into womanhood with its rigors of pain and evil as well as the counter balance of one's creativity.
- Swimming in the ocean, award of all, to heal and hold faith and to fulfill the dream of being an influence for good far away and in one's own neighborhood.

Without self-expression through beauty and nature, the heart's desire would die. Beauty and nature are integral to God showing Himself in us.

Plumeria and kukui nut lei. The lei is dark and light colored signifying being in the middle of the journey. The kukui nut is a resource for the oil used in lamps.

CHAPTER III

Hearts, Flowers, and Feathers

"When the child came toward me I saw that the box contained one remaining lei; it was broken into two pieces. She merely tied the two pieces together, gently placed the cool red plumeria around my shoulders and kissed me."

Clematis from the farm transplanted to the Apple Shed

CHAPTER III

Hearts, Flowers, and Feathers

Beauty is Central

"Learning by watching Jacque" included living life artistically—a common-life aesthetic in which forms and functions complement each other. Artistic activity necessarily includes studied forms of artful expression as well. Through a shamanistic submergence of my veneer academia adult life I surfaced to express the real longings which had been part of my young life. Were dancing, acting, singing appropriate to teen-age development but not to mature women in serious careers? Was it agility? Revisiting the forty-year-old dreams they seemed like old friends. I became transcendent because I was in touch with my true and total self, not just my mind. Expressing and serving myself rather than totally giving over to the development of others was necessary to survival. Spiritual perception came because I had chosen to be in a beautiful, natural area of the country with the historic and current influences of native peoples and I was moored in an artistic mecca of the United States. Gardening, singing, dancing, finding art in common life, and gathering talismans were literal artistic activities in which I immersed myself. Their spiritual corollaries of growing love, hearing freedom, practicing grace, and revealing my soul through gathering talismans helped me create the fulfilled life I desired. The stories which follow demonstrate the tangible substance of God in my life.

With only a trunk full of clothes, my sister and I had driven across the country in my PhD gift car from my parents. I left my home and every dear possession to find myself, ostensibly through another college teaching job which I did not want to take. Although I delight in the indulgence of telling my stories of personal courage, my hope is to influence the emergence of your artistic soul. This chapter is a Whitman's Sampler. What you do not identify with or want to taste you can put back in the box and choose another piece. See what tastes delicious.

My Halo

Mother tells me a story about when I asked her life's meaning: "Mother, why are we here on earth?"

She thoughtfully replied—"To Glorify God." I asked, "Is that like Halo glorifies your hair?" Whenever she laughingly tells me this, I feel her approval of my seriousness at a young age.

ॐ

"Mother's Day"

Excerpted from *Dancing up the Mountain,*
A Guide to Writing Your Life Story,
Jacqueline K. Kelsey, PhD, 1999

On the Sunday celebrating Mother's day, we two artists slurped lattes at the corner coffee shop. My mother was far away in the Midwest and I missed her. She had sent me $5.00 to have a latte with her. I am not sure if my friend Joseph's mother was living yet or not. He did not speak of her.

With a research degree in hand and university teaching experience behind me I was now looking for a less intellectual life, one outside the system. My workshops could hardly compare to a paid university teaching job. We two artists had transposed our gifts. Joseph, a well-known gallery artist in the past, now painted houses. Of the two of us, I was more on track but he made a living.

Our attraction to gallery hopping on Mother's Day tapped into our deep desire for artistic self-expression. Ordinarily Joseph would not have asked me to spend time with him but today I sensed he understood that I felt forlorn. Maybe he did too. He used his artistic sensitivity to nurture me; perhaps he found comfort in being with a woman.

I would have to use effort to get out of the truck cab parked too close to the curb on the steep incline up from First Street. Before I could get out, a group of men hanging on to each other slanted from the building wall and back toward the truck. A woman broke away from the pack of men and stretched from the waist up gangling her arms toward the truck. I was afraid I could not get the window rolled up in time to shield myself from her long thin arm stretching from her capped sleeve like a leafless tree limb reaching for the sun. A pale wrinkled palm pressed on the glass to steady her. Her leathery face smiled at me through her toothless cavern. I could disappear into her formlessness and I absorbed her muted, rubbery wish for me—"Happy Mother's Day." I connected with her and felt comforted in my aloneness.

She mustered the grace to reach out to me and stumble back into the group of "drunken sailors" staggering to get up the hill. I had drawn a humble servant to nurture me when my mother was far away. What a creative artist I am. And she chose me to rekindle her knowledge of being the aboriginal mother.

&

Receive Love

What I discovered in the art gallery Mecca is the beauty in peoples' loving expressions through whatever guise they escape. Relating to people had always come easy. I seemed to draw them by doing nothing. Living artistically had seemed unessential to survival. But as you can see, the only grace on Mother's Day came from a drunken woman to a bereft woman when love was given and received. The artist, the woman and I created an artistic expression of love.

Come Alive

During my creative years writing other people's life stories was easy for me. I found great value in the simplest endeavors and felt great admiration for people—a lady making soup for her family, snow sledding in the park, a daycare bus rider, buttoning his heavy coat with one hand.

However, my expectations were so high for myself that I could not see that I had achieved much and how much I loved life and nature and that I already had achieved a great deal. Actually, I had achieved so much—degrees and travel and teaching—that I was not satisfied with understanding and self expression. I needed to do more and more of the high-test runs. I admired the simplicity of others' lives.

How would I make a living? Would I recap on eight years of doctoral work? I would work my brain over a hot latte, developing sophisticated plans for workshops, hoping a purpose for life work would come through. Of course, it did not. At age fifty-five after my six-year shaman-like change, the burial and the emerging, I decided that I had lived my life fully and I could give it up. I was satisfied with my life experience. I had done enough. There was nothing more to do and perhaps I was complete. I could end life and feel fulfilled (not that I wanted to die but rather to stop achieving).

Gratefully there was and has been more. My satisfaction has seemed to come through expressing beauty rather than achieving. Beauty centers me in life.

There is always the standard for rating expression but my efforts, as in educational achievement, have not been minimal in time or variety. However, a focus from my soul has been on the love of nature as a setting for expression as well as the medium for artistry. My voice and my body have presented my limitless soul.

Beauty centers me in life because life does hold lack of beauty like pain, disappointment and death. However, they are part of the artistry of oneness of time, balance, breadth, beauty and love. Therefore, I have learned to deem all of life worthy of my attention and to shroud it in beauty. Being in the present with one event is being one with the others. I have determined to create lifework which allows me to express my beliefs and values when love shows up and continues to grow amidst flowers.

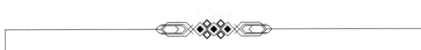

Truth is Beauty

The author's view cherishes a firm belief in the existence of another reality beyond the one we can see with our eyes and touch with our hands. Nature manifests that other reality mainly through beauty, specifically the rich beauty of flowers.

In a Platonic way, beauty existing by itself is attributed more actual existence than the world we live in. Jacqueline's conviction, expressed in a naively straight forward, matter-of-fact way leaves no room for doubt that the supernatural is at work. It requires no needless apologetic argumentation that could diminish the effect of the supernatural. With her confident point of view she is able to guide the reader onto a better level of existence by lifting him/her from a darkened emotional stage into the light and the openness of the realm that exists beyond visibility.

Thus, the reader is given not just an illustration of how to live a better life; he is moved to change his point of view of life into Plato's realm of truth.

Hans P. Dietz, PhD, Classical Scholar

Grow Love

Flowers

Gardening flowers was a quiet pursuit in the cool Northwest. Like in Alaska, flowers nodded in perfect sun and thrived in rain and cool. Meridians filled with rhododendrons and blue and pink hydrangea bushes to hush the traffic and tourist-filled sidewalks. Overflowing flower baskets swayed like women's hips in short skirts. Beauty growing everywhere, I, too, entered the spirit. The mind was not essential in the Northwest unless one worked for Microsoft. The healing vortex was native, natural, and artistic, sensuous, and fun. It was a perfect cure for my worn-out life of academia, divorce and sickness.

July steamed hot above the garage in the apartment where I lived; therefore, I went to Hawaii. Flowers would cool the natives as well as me with their cool-petaled leis. When I returned to my lake view apartment, I discovered that my landlords had built a second story deck to overlook the water. I lined the deck benches with pots of flowers. My upper story garden connected me to the beauty growing everywhere—in the village, in Alaska, in Hawaii, and in me.

Restoring myself through planting flowers has been a lifelong pattern but it was hardly a life pursuit even though my ex-husband used to predict that I would spend all the energy, time, and money to get a PhD and end up working in a flower shop. I used to relieve stress by digging dandelions before I divorced my first husband.

When I moved to a new house, my therapy for getting over the divorce was rooting and planting bushes and trees. My new husband and I created a mini-plantation. Alone again after thirteen years, I returned to being with flowers on a scale I could manage—flowers on a deck overlooking the lake bounded by mountains, far from the Midwestern cornfields.

I returned to the farm in the Midwest in the mid-nineties to establish my Illinois residence and to redirect my life. My therapy for loneliness in a small hometown was to trim and manicure the yard. I did not invade my mother's garden; rather I tried to maintain it as she wanted it. After my father died and she went into the nursing home, large old trees had to be taken down. In their places I scattered large round gardens of wild perennial seeds to take the place of grass which I thought would not catch on in the hot wind on top of the hill. I grew many small gardens to manage my grief and the stress of going to the nursing home for hours each day. On a home visit, Mother scattered a wedge of daisy seeds from her wheelchair to continue the flower circle.

During this time I commuted to the Northeast to realign with my ex-husband. He bought a house. The long gold picket fence separated the narrow mountain base lot from the street and top of the riverbank. The former resident had planted twenty-one flowerbeds. Three feet of grass along the road remained—the only place where sun shone and no other flowers grew. This would be my new perennial bed growing the length of the picket fence and as high as the fence. A grieving friend had recently planted a memory garden for her father—her entire yard was filled with yard art and tall vibrant flowers many of which she dug up and replanted along my fence. The flowers, mostly golden, delighted the neighbors and spoke out beauty and liveliness when I returned to Illinois. They told people I was still there when I had already returned to Illinois, Washington, and Hawaii. Other gardeners have come along and wanted to thin the flowers, separate them, remove and reduce them so there would be more focus on smaller plants. I love the bank of solid flowers holding in my life in the gold house along the river.

Growing flowers has grown with my life and helps me remember life events and favorite people. My father fertilized the hollyhocks we planted down at the Post House, the old water tower base, and surprised me with their quick development. He was aware of life passing quickly in his late eighties and, also, he wanted to contribute to a garden we made together. The crepe paper red, pink, and white blooms tugged on strong tall stems, flanking the shake shingle wall of the obelisk water tower—the oldest frame building in the county from the early 1820's. The picture of flowers against weathered shake shingles with him posing on his garden tractor should have been in a farm and home magazine.

When mother came to visit me in the Northwest, I remember trying to take a favorite picture of the meridian flowers—the long narrow beds would not fit into a decent picture. Like flowers, life is short even when the flowers are perennial. Flowers' lives have to be expressions for the moment and sufficient without great purpose other than to be beautiful. They are, therefore, essential. I have saved bouquets and wreaths I brought to Vermont from the Northwest. They remind me of life's continuity in the cool, relaxed living out of each day.

One of the last times I went to Hawaii I airmailed orchid leis to Mother and Dad; my brother took a great picture of our parents wearing the purple leis. We keep it out on their piano.

"Heart of Leis"

Why was I on the Big Island, I asked myself; "No highs, no lows, no experiences to mark that I had visited or been visited." I had come to Kona from Kamuela the day before, where life seemed ordinary, workaday and low-keyed.

The Big Island was known to be a place of healing and I had visited it many times to experience healing. The lady at the gift shop remarked that it was good that I had not come for any healing this time because I could receive enjoyment from what the island had to offer otherwise. Certainly I was open to having a good time. Maybe the vacuous feeling I had was openness to new experiences.

Late in the evening an attractive woman danced the hula at the restaurant near where I stayed. I was used to more beauty and heart from previous visits to Kona. The loud Hawaiian music strummed a contrast to the natural beauty of hula dancing against an ocean backdrop. The saving innocence appeared when a long-haired child swished her grass skirt among the guests as she bestowed red plumeria leis. Because I was late to the performance I was afraid there would not be a lei for me.

When the child came toward me I saw that the box contained one remaining lei; it was broken into two pieces. She merely tied the two pieces together, gently placed the cool red plumeria around my shoulders and kissed me. Earlier I had bought a yellow plumeria lei from a street stand, the only one I had ever bought. Usually I picked up fallen yellow and red flowers from under the trees along the road. With each blossom I would make a decision about how I felt, available or committed. And then I would push the blossoms under my hair over the right or left ear—single, committed.

After the outdoor show I returned to my room for a one-night stay. The faded décor stifled the air. Tomorrow would start a new day. I placed the red and yellow leis inside each other on the empty pillow next to mine; they became my company—my Aloha. As I fell asleep, at least I had given myself the reassurance of lovely fragrance.

The next morning when I scuffed toward my bedside I was awestruck by the scene. I bowed in reverence. Someone had visited me. There had been a presence next to me while I slept. The lei flowers had formed a heart. The moment I saw the heart I believed the artistic finger of the Holy Spirit had created two perfectly related hearts for me and I believed that God had showered me with love in Aloha language.

The night before I had placed the leis inside each other—the red plumeria on the inside, the yellow flowers around the outside. In the morning the petals faced toward one another in perfect symmetry with intricate spacing as if they were painted bisque flowers; no human touch could have arranged such perfection. I accepted the supernatural start of my day and moved into the rest of the day—a normal day of finding a place to sleep while I lived in Kona for a short while.

I stopped by the lobby desk of a sightseeing company in a local hotel where Hawaiians stay. When I told the clerk the story of the flowers, she explained the phenomenon easily.

"The energy of the flowers had moved themselves." The Hawaiian view was always dear to my heart.

Serendipitously, when I told her I had no place to stay in Kona, she invited me to stay in the home of a friend. The next morning I relaxed with coffee on the deck overlooking the Kona coast and listened to the friend's story about separating from her husband because she was not a focus for him; he was unable to give her the feeling of being his center of attention.

The life story paralleled with mine and explained my empty feelings. Perhaps I had come to Hawaii by myself so that I could confirm the truth. Certainly I did not want to be in Hawaii with a man who did not make me feel loved. Being by myself was better, albeit terribly lonely.

Before I left my new friend's home for the day I wanted to test to see if the flowers had really moved for me the night before and whether or not they would do it again by giving me a confirming message. How little faith I seemed to have. I re-arranged the red plumeria inside the yellow lei. I tried to make a perfect heart like the one on my pillow last night. The petals refused to lay perfectly symmetrical as they had before. The flowers' powerful energy would confirm itself for me.

I created a new arrangement. I puffed the red plumeria into the right half of the heart to picture my aloneness, my half self. At dusk I returned to my room. In amazement I saw that the red plumeria bunched together around an opening. I could see that there was a hole in my heart.

Looking back I understand that there was a deep wound and yet possibly a power not only from the flowers but also from myself, God in me, to draw into my life what I needed: love from people, places, messages, pictures, and nature. "Surely goodness and mercy follow me all the days of my life."

Several years later my partner and I returned to the Big Island for a vacation. He announced that he had lost interest in me even though he kept his commitment to take the trip. Dismayed, I heard the opposite of what I had prepared for. Nevertheless, at the end of the trip, as we drove out of Kona we decided to toss our leis into the water and read the omen of whether we would return or not dependent on the direction of the leis. Because of the rocky beaches it was a challenge to find a spot close enough to the waves. The power of my heart's desire was stronger than his words and to our surprise the two leis floated together and found each other, one inside the other. They appeared in two perfect circles.

છ

My new market friend who made and sold leis at the Saturday market.

Treasure Freedom

Song

Not only love and beauty in nature became my resurrected artistry, but also the soul's voice expressed in singing. I grew into greater freedom by hearing my own voice. "You have a beautiful voice." He said he had listened to me sing during the service. This same man had stopped me after Lenten Bible study to say that he liked the idea of intimacy which I suggested when Christ did not want to have His healing announced. Singing in the shower may be the same kind of self-healing. Because of Musical Church, I was encouraged to take group singing lessons on Saturday mornings. We would go to our singing pastor's home and sing in groups while he coached us. When my mother came to visit me for two weeks, I took her, too. She had been a member of the Chicago Symphony Chorus when she was young—and in church choirs later. All of her sisters were musical. Also, I pursued the lessons because I knew my grandmother on my father's side had sung not only in church but also in lead musical roles at the local opera house. My mother's voice, at this time in her late life, like mine was wee, barely audible. Where had we lost our voices? My dream was to sing; I knew there was voice to be heard.

After the group singing experience, I ventured into private lessons from a retired voice teacher at the local arts school. He exchanged cleaning his home for help with developing my voice. Surprisingly, he said his teacher did not allow him to sing a melody for two years. All training was for the quality of the sound. I was disappointed because I wanted to hear myself and wanted others to hear me, even though I could not have sung for anyone else. I believe the "voice" is about being listened to. I had not been listened to, for the most part, during my childhood because children "were to be seen and not heard." Incredibly my career choice was teaching with audience all day. However, I chose to plan people's learning and let them talk. I chose to be in the background much of the time. Naturally, yes? Mostly I expressed my creativity in releasing theirs. In dreaming of my afterlife I chose a new role when I did not have to serve others.

Singing is intimate, the closest vibration to one's heart. Birds have soul and sing out their hearts in beautiful sounds. In my family's farmhouse I lie in bed and feel the sun from the East as it wakes me with shadows of the old oak tree. Birds chirp me the rest of the way to open to a new day. When I try to decide "What next?" in life, I settle into the present by singing up and down the scales when I ride alone in the car along country roads.

One of my dreams is to sound beautiful to others from a stage. Unafraid, I have broken into song when I told stories. I liked the way I sounded. When I started voice lessons again at the local college in the Midwest I told my teacher I would like to sing cabaret—how unlikely for me. Probably it is a romanticized version of being listened to, because it creates an intimate audience compared to being on stage. What is my dream? Somehow if I do not sing for others I will feel I have missed out on developing one of my gifts. Is it not like the tree falling? If it is not heard how will it give testimony? There is discipline in singing and probably that is what has stopped. What a delight when I learned the difference between letting breath flow and controlling breathing. Perhaps the hope for me in life is to sing and to let go—freedom.

Going to a singing camp in the wild, on an island—how perfect. I learned to tone—to let my voice go, my soul free. Outside my tent I lay on the ground surrounded by compassionate singers who assisted in "the song," in a shaman-like burial of self. I reached a high note in me that did not exist before. Getting to it was left up to me while they listened. The weekend wafted away in "toning" song in the farm chapel and in dance amidst Sufi movements in the field.

Au naturel, we took in only what was healthy in vegetarian food and we surrounded ourselves in fun conversation with lots of laughter.

When I was teaching in a college, I tried to transfer my newfound freedom to a class of mature teachers who sat on the floor with me and toned a bit. It seemed appropriate to the learning goal for the day: expressing oneself and hearing the voices of others. However, I was admonished by the department chair not to tone again because one of the students complained. Therefore, I joined the monks for early morning prayers and chanting, the only environment where I could breathe. This experience was not unlike leaving out literature in my survey course when it offended a sensitive student in the conservative religious school where I had taught for four years. I even removed the text from my shelf when board members came to visit in the spring. Most of the time I start workshops with singing my theme song; "Open my eyes that I may see glimpses of truth… (Clara Scott pub.1885)"

Rural hymn singing, the old-fashioned kind, soulfully "belted out" moves me more than "The Church is One Foundation." Tent meetings and revivals join the crowd in a fervor of true, common beliefs. As a teen-ager and young married camp counselor, I loved to lose myself up to my eyebrows in the crowd yelling, "There's Power in the Blood" or "Bringing in the Sheaves."

Better yet are the country songs we played on the jukebox in the local cafés. We crooned on Saturday nights when my folks took us to hoe-down gatherings in country towns within fifteen miles of my hometown. Gospel and country, banjo, homemade instruments, and harmonica remind me that I am from the near south. Sunday afternoons we still gather in a country town at the roadside general store; twenty or so neighborhood musicians play and sing. We tap and hum.

My Dulcimer

The Arkansas folk singer invited us for Sunday breakfast at the local café. His Native American wife told us his life story of loss and singing. We had driven several hundred miles to meet him, an award recipient from a national teacher's organization for his innovative use of music to teach social studies.

He still performed in a Saturday night barn program featuring his name, a small testimony to his influence on the music community in the valley.

In town on the square where musicians gathered on weekend nights, he guided me to the dulcimer shop and to the hand-made walnut instrument I sing with, playing old hymns by ear like drifting into far away times when people transported themselves to the heart of place from which they came—the drone of the bagpipe background reminding them of Scotland through their migration melodies.

&

When my father died, we celebrated his life at a country church called "Campground." The story goes it was near a Civil War campground for soldiers. Most of my mother's Scottish Andrews ancestors are buried in the church cemetery. Mother and Dad and our whole family would go to church when we came home to visit. Dad's dream was to support the little church so that it could be filled. Indeed at his service the church was filled and we sang many old songs a cappella, including "There's a Church in the Valley by the Wildwood." My dad was a great banjo player and like others in the family had a beautiful tenor voice. He sang along with his banjo playing. Certainly, he would have appreciated the song service. An old-fashioned outdoor buffet followed in the churchyard shaded by large old tree canopies, like in a Norman Rockwell painting. Song and food for the soul to join this life with Heaven.

Treasure Freedom

Like birds our souls are free. We sing to greet and end the day. Not all flight leads to freedom. We also sing when injury is the destiny. Birds fly into the picture windows of my parents' farm home in the Midwest. The birds see the light from the windows on the opposite side of the living room and believe there is a clear flight path.

In October I had returned to my second home in the East. Actually, I had come to my Vermont home to rest before making my next move.

Never had a bird flown into the storm door of the restored old house in the Northwoods, with the mountain behind and the river in front. The light behind the front storm door created an illusion of freedom for the bird just as my beautifully restored home created the illusion of a nest for me.

Dad's bird feeder in front of the picture windows of our family's farm home.

Evening Song

Kathryn and John ordinarily would build a fire in the wood stove and eat soup and sandwiches on TV trays in front of the living room fire. Tonight they sat at the kitchen table for supper. Outside the evening was warm, like summer leaves floating down among the dried flower stalks. The tall black wooden door propped open to cool off the house but the glass storm door had been put in for the winter.

Kathryn had to drive twelve miles to get to song practice by 6:30; it was already 6:00 o'clock. She shot up from the table at 6:20 knowing it was too late. The drive through the country took twenty minutes to arrive at the rural village where the group practiced in the community building. Running through the dining room, she grabbed her sweater off the door peg because the air would cool down after practice. Fall evenings in the Northwoods were chilly.

She pushed herself through the front storm door sideways and stepped hard onto the blue front porch carpet. The yellow bug light created an eerie fall night. Her knees locked when she stopped herself abruptly. She could not take another step. On the blue carpet beneath the tall black door lay a taupe-colored bird the size of a model airplane—tilted back on its side, with its wing straight up; it had crash-landed. Its long beak pointed straight up. The wide-open eye stared, trance-like.

She stared at its chest to see if it breathed. "Was it alive?" Kathryn wondered. Gently, "in and out," the soft feathers lay easily on its speckled breast. In and out, in and out, the soft feathers gave way to its automatic breathing. John was at the kitchen table. Kathryn raced into the kitchen to forewarn him. He said he had heard the sound of it hitting the glass.

Out the kitchen door to the woodshed, she searched for a container, shoe box size, and sent John into the side yard to grab hands full of leaves to fill the box. "Hurry," she called, while she tore off a paper towel on the kitchen counter and urged John to the front porch with her. The upstairs hall light filled the narrow staircase passage behind them and glowed against the storm door glass.

Kathryn instructed John to fill the shoebox with leaves. She could not touch the bird. Feeling the wild life in her hand was too intimate. Perhaps it was the fear of feeling death that made her dig her elbows into her ribs. "No." She shook her hands.

John did not seem to mind. The paper towel would create a barrier to the life or death inside. The bird felt John's hand closing around it. When John set the bird on the blue rug, the bird shifted its head upright. Its beak pointed forward. Kathryn could see that the bird looked alert, like always. Still holding lightly, John moved his arm, crane-like, from the middle of the blue carpet toward the shoebox, pushed up against the balustrade to steady it. As he lowered his stiff crane arm, Kathryn noticed that the towel would be under the bird's feet and a larger corner would be left over. She wanted to cover the bird so it would feel secure. The half-opened eyelids shut out the light and the pain. Kathryn reverently knelt next to the shoebox. Quietly, she watched the motionless bird. It looked severely injured—no longer dazed, but rather overcome by the pain holding it still.

Kathryn knew that she was only human help; she had called on all her childhood know-how. "Shoeboxes were good for most houses—cards for school chum on Valentine's Day, miniature doll house, dioramas, and burial chambers." Supper had been rushed, and the bird was dying. She was already late for singing practice. Leaning against the balustrade, her mind whispered, "How can I leave the bird?" The patient bird had accepted the shoebox and even the paper towel. "What could she do?"

She noticed the green words printed on the paper towel: "Health and Happiness." Her only assist, she spoke the words like they were a benediction, not knowing what good they would do. Would her words heal a bird? Kathryn felt better when she could do something that she knew would help. She knew it would not help to sit with the bird and felt that she had to keep her commitment to herself to sing.

When she arrived at the basement of the community building the group stopped singing to welcome Kathryn. She explained that a bird had flown into the storm door and she took time to nest it in a box with leaves and a paper towel over it. The ladies smiled sympathetically, when she recounted the "health and happiness" message tilting their heads knowingly. What did they know? After the harmony began, she forgot about the bird. She would not have to face knowing about the bird's fate until she climbed the porch steps leading to the tall black door.

On the drive home she had felt calm. John, too, had gone to a choir rehearsal. She knew song lifts. It was magical when she felt lighter after singing with the ladies. She wondered about how John felt singing in the bass section. He too would have to face knowing about the injured bird. Before leaving John had shut the wooden door so no light from the hall would shine through the storm door. No other birds would fly into the see-through glass. The porch was dark.

Standing for a moment on the top step. Kathryn dreaded lifting the paper towel to see whether or not the bird would be dead or would have flown away. From the steps she could see the "Health and Happiness" towel was half over the damp leaves. Kathryn kneeled down next to the balustrade as if she were in prayer. Carefully, lifting the damp corner tip of the towel, she saw that the bird had moved; white and gray droppings dotted the white paper. The bird must have heard her song; it had refueled and lifted. It was well enough to take off—to fly away—a miracle in her spirit.

When John came home at 8:00 o'clock, she met him at the gate. "How was song practice?" John asked. How could he not remember to ask about the bird first of all? Perhaps he had avoided thinking about the bird. Annoyed, she kept a solemn face. "You'll have to look for yourself," she spurted out. He too saw dark droppings on the white towel. John was silent for a moment. When he lifted the towel he exclaimed, "How was song practice?" Kathryn hummed, "I told the women about the bird."

Kathryn and John shivered on the top step while mulling over the bird's takeoff. The cold night air banked around the porch. "How was your rehearsal?" asked Kathryn, wondering if he would give a clue to his feelings. "Wonderful. The bass section always lifts the sopranos. We support the whole choir." Kathryn knew he felt important. Perhaps he would realize that he, too, helped the bird to fly away.

80

The Bold Limitless Flight

While in the East, I gave fireside readings after dinner at a White Mountain hotel. The program of poetry to which I invited guests who read with me presents *Freedom of Song in the Flight of the Bird*. From the beauty of nature I found instruction and solace to parallel my life depicted in Robert Frost's poetry whose farm was nearby. The text is typed out on the following page.

The Mount Washington
Hotel & Resort
presents

The Bold Limitless Flight
Poems by Robert Frost

Presented by Dr. Jacqueline K. Kelsey
December 3, 2001

Part I On the Path
Bravado
A Serious Step Lightly Taken
The Road Not Taken

Part II The Dark and the Light
The Night Light
Away
In a Glass of Cider

Part III Faith
Questioning Faces
Winter Eden
Innate Helium
"May I Come In" said the Sparrow
from Beneath the Tall Black Door by Dr. Jacqueline K. Kelsey

Part IV Relationships
A Time to Talk
Bereft
In Hardwood Groves
Tree at my Window

Part V Life
A Steeple
On a Tree Fallen Across the Road
Stopping by the Woods on a Snowy Evening

Dr. Jacqueline Kelsey is a teacher, writer, and workshop leader on *Writing Your Life Story*. Through creative interpretation of American Classic authors, she encourages the audience's creative expression; she leads them to consider greater life fulfillment.

Arts for Life   (802) 757-8062

The Bold Limitless Flight
Poems by Robert Frost

Presented by Dr. Jacqueline K. Kelsey
December 3, 2001

Part I On the Path

Bravado
A Serious Step Lightly Taken
The Road Not Taken

Part II The Dark and the Light

The Night Light
Away
In a Glass of Cider

Part III Faith

Questioning Faces
Winter Eden
Inate Helium
"May I Come In" said the Sparrow
from <u>Beneath the Tall Black Door</u> by Jacqueline K. Kelsey

Part IV Relationships

A Time to Talk
Bereft
On a Tree Fallen Across the Road
Stopping by the Woods on a Snowy Evening

Dr. Kelsey is a teacher, writer and workshop leader on Writing
Your Lifestory. Through creative interpretation of American
classic authors she encourages audience's creative expression.
This leads them to consider greater life fulfillment.

We are all in flight, in the air; the manual for the long journey is learned from injury, love, beauty, grace, freedom and space, and the soul's spirit.

John and Kathryn Kelsey used the woods and fields to protect and preserve wildlife.

Plumicorn's Flight

"Ewa-Yea little owlet" sang Hiawatha's grandmother as she looked into the baby's eyes, golden owlet eyes. She rocked the baby with lullaby as she cried over his mother's death in the story by Longfellow, "Song of Hiawatha." Two owlets: Hiawatha and Plumicorn.

Too strong for the Red Hawk's stick nest, the early spring wind tossed and rolled the nest off the limb onto the ground. "Plumicorn" huddled in the center of the feathers hoping to stay warm but there was no life—no sound from the other chicks.

In the early morning a county ranger walked the fence line and into the woods to check on injured animals. In the safety of the trees in the isolated woods the male and female owl had chosen to nest high in a tree. The fallen nest lay quiet in the clear air. Gateway Farm's woods had always served as a preserve for wild animals.

The ranger carefully stepped deeper into the haven of trees. She was a careful observer of tracks and disturbed foliage. Quickly she spied the nest on the ground beneath the tall tree. Coming close, she could see the one live owlet hovering. He was young but she could see his tufted ears, his "plumicorns." He would not fly for six weeks. The father owl had left pieces of squirrel and small bird in the nest for the three owlets and their mother to eat.

How would the ranger help this totally dependent creature? Ordinarily in the wild an owlet would depend on his parents for a year. How could it survive and grow to adult maturity so that it could mate? The ranger connected the owl with a long-time friend to injured animals who took the owl to a rescue shelter for injured wild animals located about fifty minutes away. In a tall wire pen the owl learned to fly. It would be a full year until he was fully grown and could be safe to return to the wild.

For over fifty years the woods at Gateway Farm, and its family, the Kelsey's, had protected and nurtured many creatures. Kathryn Kelsey wanted it to be a preserve forever. There was no hunting allowed. Deer, fox, hawks, crows, raccoons, and coyotes inhabited the woods and its pond. John kept the frozen pond broken up because family horses lived in the old barn and its paddock as well as the woods. Family picnics and school outings co-existed with the wildlife. It was a sanctuary even though a natural balance of life maintained itself. Wildflowers and mushrooms abounded. A new layer of wild life had built up over time amidst the walnuts in the former cow pasture of the Andrews' dairy farm.

Always an advocate for animals, Jacque met with the local animal protector on occasion to save an animal. The most recent phone talk over a small hawk on the Civil War statue at the courthouse led the two to meet and talk over the need to return the owl to the woods where he came from. The man had always worked with her father to use the farm woods for animals needing a home.

The night was chosen—a clear bright moon softened the night surrounding the top of the hill where field weeds swayed in early spring. The family and friends gathered at the end of the circle drive near the house with the woods in view. The caretaker couple brought the large wire cage out of their truck. His wife had come along to chronicle the event in pictures and put it on the local radio station. Kathryn pulled her wheel chair near to the edge of the drive. The family who lived at Gateway moved in closer to make the circle.

When the caretaker pulled the three-foot bird from its cage, the Great Horned Owl with its "plumicorn" ear tufts panned the group with its easily mobile head. His golden eyes blinked as he took in his witnesses and transfixed his own grand wild being. The caretaker held firmly to the owl's strong legs supporting him on his arm with heavy cuffed gloves. "Plumicorn"leaned and teetered into the direction and night air of his new freedom.

We saw his wisdom, knew his intelligence. As he banked into takeoff with a five-foot wingspread, we heard and felt the whir taking our longings and spirit with him. We had met the Divine in creation, silently flying into the dark. The moon's light reassured us that he would not be swallowed up. He would provide his own food and carve out a life in solitude for a while because he had no group. He would mate and become a father to owlets, letting them depend on him for as long as he had lived.

A long life ahead, he would provide inspiration and he would be seen for the next thirty years, as long as Jacque would live, were she to live as long as her ninety-six year old mother, who had nurtured her Gateway Farm sanctuary for wildlife.

&

Dance Fan
Dance of Life
Chosen for Honor
Passing Down the Feathers
Teaching the Dance

Practice Grace

Dance

All stories excerpted from *Keeper of the Sacred*
Jacqueline K. Kelsey, PhD, 1994 (unpublished)

Dance Fan

Telling children stories and teaching them acrobatics created close bonds for me when I was young. As with animals, I connected with them early in their lives and mine. Similarly, at a powwow I bought rattles and dance fans from vendors and gave them to children to play with at the side of the dance floor. Their fans drew attention!

It seemed I was one of few non-native American people at the powwow. My self-styled regalia, of leather pants to represent leggings, showed from under a long, bright blue skirt with geometric design; a purple suede fringed collar covered my shoulders. I marked time with a small brown bird's-wing dance feather. One of my new vendor purchases, it was humble looking because it was small but I loved it.

At the announcement of "inter-tribal" I joined and circled the gym floor. A beautiful Native American girl dressed in white regalia led the dances. After the dance, she came to me and asked if she could carry my dance fan. We connected and honored each other. Her fan was large and beautifully made with white feathers.

She too, like the children, wanted to have something from me. I received her blessing—knowing about me or my soul from the dance.

ଞ

Riding a horse at the Dells, Wisconsin

Dance of Life

The drumbeat signaled me to crouch. Elbows close to my body, weaseling through the crowd towering above me, I arrived just in time for the color guard. A Native American observed me from across the powwow dance floor. Our expressionless eyes met without either of us giving recognition to the other. Nonetheless, we had acknowledged each other. No response was necessary. Actually, I let him teach me at this moment.

I felt like a grouse that he was when he danced, circling at a tilt, feathered wings hanging down toward the earth. Crouching down, I had to crook my head to look up at the flag. I had the same feeling when I first felt like a fish, snorkeling in Keauhou Bay on the Big Island. No longer could I breathe as a human being. Rather, I had to breathe under water like a fish, albeit through a tube rather than through my gills. The breathing created me into a fish, a pre-state so that I splayed my fin feet and curved my knees to bend my body in half and swam as a fish with the fish. Becoming a natural creature was familiar to me.

Higher up in the middle of the gym bleachers, a small Native woman sat by herself and I joined her. The two of us, alone, waited for the inter-tribal dance announcement which meant I could join in the dance. With her arms folded, she slightly bent forward, staring straight ahead. After a few minutes of silence, she softly spoke unimpassioned words to announce herself, "I am a Princess; I am a daughter of the Chief." I, too, heard my own announcement, "I am a grouse, I am a fish, and I am a Native." Soon I would show this to the tribe while receiving an unexpected place of honor during the evening ceremony.

When pointing to her headband, the Native woman explained that it was made of cedar. The band showed me that she was a princess. I asked her if she would like to dance. There was no answer, no movement. After a few moments, while looking straight ahead, she came alive, bounced up and spoke words with her whole body, "Let's go!"

∞

Arm in arm, we climbed down ten flights of bleachers onto the gym floor. We circled the gym floor three times. There were no words shared, only silence typical of women, Native dancers. Like with my Native American friend, only recognition of each other seemed necessary. Each time we circled the huge gym floor and came to the place where we could return to our seats, she looked straight ahead and continued to shuffle to the drum beat. After the third round, we returned to our perches. She turned to me and announced, "Today, my grandson said, 'Grandma, you need a new feather,' and so he bought me a new feather," turning her head to the side so I could see the feather in her headband. Slowly she faced the gymnasium dance floor again, looking straight ahead and re-announced, "I am a Princess; I am the daughter of the Chief." I quietly moved away and climbed down the bleacher planks to rejoin the Native women below.

ॐ

Chosen for Honor

While we women sat in the bleachers the evening host came over to us and asked the friend next to me to dance. She turned him down and when he had turned away, she whispered, covering her mouth to my ear, "he might want more." He came over to me and asked me to dance. Did he think I was a Native?

The families gathered to be received by the host and stood in two long rows, from the bleachers, to the back of the gym. I knew these people because I had come to powwows for two years by myself, dancing as they did. As the host and I walked onto the floor, near the families and children who had gathered in the center, he explained that his wife had died and he wanted a partner during this ceremony when the children would receive feathers by more experienced, older "young" people.

Wearing my long, leather pants to look like leggings, I covered them with a bright, blue gathered skirt, with rows of geometric designs which my mother had given me for my birthday. Always, I covered my shoulders, usually with a suede-fringed collar, which I bought in Arkansas. And of course, I wore my moccasins. For my lifetime I had wanted a pair. Every family vacation we took to Oklahoma, Wisconsin, or Texas, I wanted moccasins but I never got them. Finally at middle age, I had bought a pair of blue, red, and orange beaded moccasins at a powwow in Olympia. They were made by a Native American craftsman verified by his card from the shop—"authenticity of the source."

The host and I began at the far end of the double row, slowly padding feet to the heartbeat of the drum. When the drum was silent, we extended our right hand to each parent or friend, first he, and then I. It was a solemn occasion. When acquaintances looked at me in the eye, I was in their midst, as their equal. We had to accept each other, if for only this occasion. The Native host had elevated me with no knowledge of the need, or my past. The air was still. It seemed that he had offered me a measure of community acceptance through relationship to him.

In retrospect, I felt the same still air, the same moment of bringing home to me my great accomplishment, when I was centered in the line walking to the podium to receive my PhD diploma. The auditorium, the lights and the crowd of people were numbed into the background. I would receive my honor for jumping all of the hoops of research and diligence and self-sacrifice to get my doctorate. In regalia, I walked, two-by-two, from a holding tunnel, into the open space. That entry breakthrough when air and sound changed and I became aware of my own greatness, I allowed myself to feel it.

My Native American friends in the two columns widened their eyes to recognize that it was I, and to let me know how important the event was. There was even a nod of the head, like, "Oh-h-h." I received their honor. Taking the host aside, I told him that I felt honored because he had chosen me. Ordained for me by a Native American woman at a church retreat several months earlier, I fulfilled being "the bridge." I was privileged to receive the opportunity from them during the "passing down of feathers."

ॐ

Passing Down the Feathers

It had been my desire to find an eagle's feather because there were four eagles that lived and nested in the wooded yard near my house: two juveniles and two mature eagles. I thought, 'Surely, I could receive one.' That would have been a great honor.

Early the next morning, after making the wish, I looked out on the meadow next to the house and it seemed to me that I saw a huge feather! I was so shocked that I could not move away from the second story picture window to do what was necessary to check it out—I just squinted to see better. After getting my composure, I was willing to take the risk of the feather not being the one I had asked for. In my housecoat, while the dew was still on the grass, I slipped down the highly polished wooden stairs.

As I neared the rock wall at the edge of the yard, I saw that the feather was two—one and a second one crossed; it had not been possible for me to see that there were two making a bigger one. As I looked around me, I realized that there were not only two very large feathers, but there was a host of feathers. The entire field was covered with feathers! Although I did not get my request of the eagle's feather, I received an abundance of feathers to honor my desire and request.

It was an unusual event and was marked as such by a witness. Next-door, separated by a field lived the lawyer whose gardener had worked for him many years. Later that day when the sun had come out and the gardener was working along the stream, I went over to talk with him and told him about the incident. With amazement he, too, had seen the blanket of feathers. He said in all the years that he had worked in the yard he had never seen the field covered with feathers.

There is every reason for it to have been covered with feathers! The Canadian geese loved the field. I had watched these geese, talked to them from my deck when there were many mothers with different stages of little goslings to welcome each spring. But never, in the six years I had lived there, had I seen such a demonstration. Receiving feathers like grace gives us practice in our "dance of life." The scripture teaches, 'Ask and you shall receive' and you will receive abundantly. Thank you, God. Amen.

ॐ

Teaching the Dance

When first going to the island community, I learned that she knew about everyone and everything. She was the person to ask. Meeting her would be important to me, I thought. Several times we talked by phone, chitchatting, getting to know each other. The vendors positioned around the gym floor of the tribal center. Near the entrance doors my new friend had set up her card table. For the sale she had brought iced M&M cupcakes. I sat behind the craft vendors along the sidelines. I could hear and watch the drummers and singers. At the announcement of an inter-tribal dance I trekked over to my friend's cupcake table to ask her if we could dance together. She said she did not feel well and would watch. So, I also decided to watch from the sideline. She must have received a spark because very soon I saw her padding slowly around the circle in her worn slippers. Arm in arm she kept beat with the drum and her partner, a slightly-bent tall, thin young man. She helped him coordinate with her as she led out. It was clear to me that my old friend was offering herself as an older tribe member to assist the young in learning tribal ways, in the tradition of the life-giving celebration of the dance. He could feel belonging. Later, not long after our conversation during which she encouraged me to come to the powwow, I learned that she had passed on.

℣

Humility

- Accepting undeserved merit is a difficult battle with pride but I experienced watching it repeatedly with birds injured in flight and learned the necessity of receiving grace.
- Recently, I had been reading about healing by using the word "grace." A bird had hit the living room picture window and lay inert. I had watched my father pick up the dazed birds and warm them in his gloved hands.
- Because it was cold, I did not go outside; I tried my faith at healing from a distance through the glass. As I slowly spoke the word "grace," gradually with each repetition of blessing it raised its head until it was upright. It was like seeing a ballet dancer's neck gracefully arch under a swan's wing.

Decorate
Photograph
Paint
Act

Reveal Soul

Common-life Art

The stories of art and common life art both reveal my dependency on expression and sharing. My soul requires beauty around me. I seemed to need the most healing during the years when I was midway through life. I concentrated on non-cerebral activity to get out of my head after eight years of advanced graduate work and a twenty-two year teaching career. In most cases I had started to sing, dance or act when I was young but left it off for college and young married life and a career.

The common life art expressions more related to setting up home and having hobbies I pulled out again in concentrated form to immerse myself in a "common life" artful environment. Remembering family through their artifacts connected me to a nurturing support system. Beautiful surroundings and close family always have been touchstones for who I am. I reminded myself that my soul does not live in a vacuum.

Studied art and common life art have increased over the last twenty years since I started to soar. They are obvious parts of my long distance flight; they fly with me and help define my flight pattern of serendipitous living.

Five generations lived on the foundation of my great-great grandmother's home. The first was born in the late 1700s and died at age 98. "Grandma" is the first relative in our family cemetery.

Decorate Myself and Story telling

Hearing and visualizing life compete for my attention. At a season for chorales and caroling, this Christmas, I decided to express myself through the decorating—decorating myself instead of the house. I laid out all holiday finery on my father's bed—interesting because years ago Mother and I used to shop in the city and come home to give a style show. During my "decorating" each day I chose a new holiday look from the jewelry and blouses and scarves. The new look corresponded to the emphasis on me in telling the story as well. At this holiday, instead of listening to others' stories I created five opportunities to tell stories extemporaneously. During the season a local florist featured stories as part of the uptown holiday walk and asked me to be a storyteller in her shop for the evening. Parents circled around children who cozied on floor pillows.

ಏ

Great grandmother
in her finery
late 1800's

Clothes in Vermont Versus My Mother's Midwestern Wardrobe

Clothes have always been important to me; my mother was a fine dresser and as my sister commented at her daughter's shower at the Ritz in Chicago, "The Kelsey women always dress well." My mother's clothes were tasteful and elegant; she dressed up every day. When she taught English, her students delighted in her leather heels and gold charm bracelet. I am casual, most of the time, use good taste and love an artsy look. It gives me pleasure to combine new outfits and to feel like I have enough choices, after all. What I love about my Northwood's life is that I have so few clothes in my closet that I have to create new looks with older items. Jeans and layered sweaters suit me.

Cross Country Clothes

Change in jewelry and hats are a must—purple felt and sheepskin from the Northwest and green wool from the Green Mountains. Today at the general store in the town center the deli cook complimented me on my "purple bonnet." When I moved cross-country I took only a few clothes with me. I built a new wardrobe when I arrived, from upscale shops in the sailing village. A bonanza of clothes suited me for selling perfume during the holidays at a major department store. When I returned to the Midwest after six years I gave away beautiful woolens, the kind I love—long skirts, jersey tops, designer capes and long jackets.

During graduate school days I learned to forage for clothes and furniture in order to build my home décor. A mobile population in a university town creates many sales. The merchandise was auction quality rather than garage sale variety. I was used to antiques from my family generations back so I knew quality and chose tastefully.

Creating beauty around me and on my back has been my style; it is genetic, I am sure. My great-grandmother was a milliner. My grandmother was an artist seamstress for her five daughters. When I moved to the East, I learned that an artist lived in my sixth great grandmother's house in New Hampshire, perhaps, my sixth great grandmother was an artist? My father's mother was a talented still life and landscape painter, as well as a china painter.

೫

Photograph

Seeing life pictorially is a tradition passed on in my father's photography hobby and in the family scrapbooks. We have a storehouse of family pictures from father's family six generations back. My mother also kept up well with both sides of her family and her "original family of five sisters," as well as the farmhouse of her grandparents. Because they were poor farmers and pioneers there are no pictures beyond the third generation.

She made a scrapbook of my life and gave it to me as a gift when I was in my forties. Years ago, I saw her family portrait scrapbook of "those who have gone before."

When Dad No Longer Ventured

When Dad no longer ventured on foot around the farm, he photographed favorite political figures on TV news casts. I too have an artist's eye. Special projects come from being inspired by natural beauty around the farm fields and woods in summer. Landscape remnants of the pioneer farm roads and buildings excite me. In the woods I delight in the configurations of fallen trees and deer trails in the snow across the fields. I do not make scrapbooks; I fill shoeboxes with pictures. My photos of our storybook house in Vermont inspired illustrating the book *Beneath the Tall Black Door*, seven parables of wild animals in our home and yard.

ॐ

Photos, handwork and painting preserve perspective and expand my life over time. I surround myself wherever I have lived with my family world. It allows me comfort to expand into my community and the world at large. However, when I moved to the Northwest to come "out of the ground" I had taken nothing with me and I had to become my own world without family. This was healing in order to see on my own. It freed me.

ॐ

My Artful Surroundings

☆ The black and red needle point Japanese woman centered on the fireplace mantel

☆ A painted strawberry plant plate on a high shelf in the hutch

☆ The family's "dress pieces quilt" draped on the bedroom door

☆ The framed crewel Victorian house placed at the entrance to the living room

☆ My Grandmother's oil painting of roses above my bed

☆ The Woman at the Well painting in the dining room near the window

☆ My Aunt Jenny's Chinese bowls, plates, and vases, gifts

to her while she was a missionary in Chinatown in Chicago.

Instead of doing handwork like my two grandmothers—sewing, quilting, crewel and china painting—I collect, preserve, and use their beautiful creations throughout my home for personal treasuring of the people I love. It is healing to connect with their artistic souls. I see with their perspectives.

Grandma and Grandpa at home in their living room, a favorite place to visit for laughter and nurturing.

Paint

Instead of being a wonderful cook like my mother and grandmothers, I write my nourishing life in story. I also draw the stories when I do not have time or inclination to write. When my sister had a cancer operation several years ago, I stayed at home with her for three weeks during recovery. We walked daily in the ravine down to Lake Michigan.

When she rested, I painted my stories. Like living life, I did not know how but I just started and the images came and connected. First I drew in pencil on 8 by 11 inch art paper. The next step was to pat out the squares of color from children's water colors in a long tin black box like I did in first grade, in the same village where I visited my sister.

After the two weeks, my cousin came to visit and my sister proudly showed her the painted sketches. There was little to say about them and no one did; how embarrassing. They serve to remind me of my artful life. So I framed each one and now they hang in the "Apple Shed," my storytelling center.

ॐ

Act

I had been an actress all of my life—in grade school, high school and college, playing roles and directing one-acts and community pageants. As an adult, I would use what I knew how to do.

Making commercials could earn money. So I tried. Unlike theatre, the work was not expressive but rather highly prescriptive and economical in expression and actions. I did not get to first base. However, the woman in charge knew a drama coach who took me on for acting lessons. What a boost to my morale. He thought I was a natural and he caught on quickly to my being a ham. A terror to me was that he cast me in middle-age roles, of course, because I was fifty. However, inside I was much younger spirited than the roles in which I was cast.

In film acting classes for eight weeks, I learned to understand my emotional expression; because I was so expressive it was exaggerated on film as in life. I could see it on film. How precise each gesture and move is for the camera in contrast with stage acting. Having been in a lot of plays in high school, when I went to college my goal was to major in theatre like my sister. Due to an imbalanced life being "on the stage," my grades suffered and I returned to my hometown college which only allowed Shakespeare in a drama class. I sublimated my desires for acting to radio broadcasting and worked in the college radio station.

Have I been dramatic all my life? I carry on and entertain people at social events because of quick wit or during unseemly situations like doctor's appointments. And there was the great show in the city council meeting when I protested the land developer's placement of three multi-family dwellings next to our field and woods. I got a standing ovation and afterwards the state representative sat next to me with his arm around me to show his favor to the council.

Unlike high school teaching when I smiled my way through, I lived in a small town where I was an open book. Everyone knew when I did not show up for coffee in the local café. People tended to keep track of me when I went to church and knew where I parked my car. Therefore it was a great boon to tell a story at the local theatre last spring and remember that I was the fox, a symbol of craftiness and creativity in the story, "Paradise Climb," from *Dancing up the Mountain.* As a local boy said, I was foxy when young and now I was a gray fox.

Watching the Loretta Young show when I was a teenager, I melted into her flowing gowns and cushioned voice. Her doe eyes and flowing hair wrapped me in a silk cocoon of softness for life. I have always wanted my own television show on which I could tell soothing stories like she did and be a source of comfort. Perhaps I am able to offer a comforting voice through my storytelling. Recently an activity director in a nursing home purchased my CD *Listening in the Moment to Timeless Folks* to play for people who were dying because she said my voice would be soothing.

౩

Gather Talismans

Artifacts

Story in life's artifacts preserves and predicts valued experiences. Talismans carry Spirit. They produce innocuous effects. I believe my heart's desire for a whole life came from the tangibles which prompted me to aspire to have heart, to flower, and to fly. One has to take off from somewhere—a touchable, concrete pad.

To translate mere spirit into the everyday is to manifest or allow life to show me, what is interior as far as my heart's desires for health, wealth, relationships, and creative expression—the Four Squares which Florence Schinn presents in her book *The Game of Life and How to Play It*.

I gain by seeing the spiritual through the physical which is the mother of connection. However, I do not find it necessary to interpret great significance in all I see. Rather, I fully experience and love it. By loving it, the experience becomes translucent/spiritual. For example, when I took my mother strawberry picking for the first time when she was eighty-five and made custard for my Dad, years after his mother had died, I felt complete because I helped them experience what they loved. However, sometimes the mystical jumps out as in the story below.

Thomas—Indoors and Out

Thomas Aquinas, our long-haired farm cat, was a wild one, lived outdoors and slept in the garage in a wheel barrow set under a hanging light which my Dad fixed for him. I tamed him for indoor life as well. In the morning he sat on my mother's lap when she meditated while looking out over the farm hill.

☙

Thomas with me.

Thomas, the Psychic

In the glow of the fireplace light at night I rested in the red leather chair and Thomas wrapped himself around my head. Once, when I rested in my Dad's red leather chair, thinking about Jamie Sam's Native American book on animal medicine, I recalled a lynx description I had read earlier in the day. Immediately, Tommy bounded into my lap and laid his head on my chest. I recognized and accepted the connection between thought and action—the Supernatural at work. When my mother had to go to the nursing home, I was lying in bed at home crying over her fate. Tommy repeatedly circled the parameters of my mattress, next to my body until I reached a calm state. I knew he had ministered to me.

છ

Red Wooden Doll Chest
My Formals
The Dough Box
The Nutmeat Grinder
Grandpa Wheeler's Eyecup

Anecdotal Stories

The anecdotal stories about artifacts which follow have been selected from my life stories because they store my possessions and preserve their values. Each story represents experience the meaning of which I cannot photograph. Behind the material object there is my experience with a person connecting their values to me and my values. I write about the intangible stored in artifacts.

ꙮ

Red Wooden Doll Chest

My red wooden doll chest was the most special gift I received when I was a young child. It seemed we were poor and that I would not be able to get an expensive doll item.

Early on Christmas morning I sneaked down with my brother (two years younger) and saw the red chest with leather handles. Amazed, I remember wondering how my parents could come up with the money. It seemed that my belief in Santa was bolstered. The chest is stored on the utility room shelf at Gateway along with a crate box dollhouse my Grandfather Kelsey made for me.

ꙮ

We were at the age to still believe in Santa.

My Formals

When I graduated from eighth grade, we celebrated with a class dance and party. Mother wanted to make my dress and she let me design it. It was quite elaborate: a strapless look with a halter cuff around my neck. The skirt had a pleated insert down the front with scalloped edges—pink net pleats inset under the pink flowered skirt and embroidered bodice. When I changed the straight line to scallops, poor mother was up all night finishing it. I was scared and she reassured me she would finish. I bet she wondered, although she kept calm. Mother was full-time foreman of the sewing room at the glove factory. I imagine her professional experience with deadlines helped.

&

I wore my graduation dress to a Chicago-area
wedding of a family friend of Grandma's.

The Dough Box

The oiled wood, three-and-a-half foot box was a gift to me from my mother. When I got a divorce from my first husband, my mother took me on a trip to Galena, Illinois to soothe my soul. Since then the dough box has been a coffee table in my many living rooms. Over the years, I have stacked documents, letters, and large pictures. There is no order. I just lift the lid and slide the item under the end of the lid. It is so easy to have my print treasures together.

ॐ

The Nutmeat Grinder

Grandma Kelsey was a treasure and she freely gave her belongings to her grandchildren. When I got married, she gave me many kitchen gifts—aprons, dishes and gadgets. My favorite is a glass jar with a nut meat grinder in the lid. I have used the round jar for forty years and always think of my grandmother's love of cooking, love of home and garden, love of family and animals, and love of laughter.

ॐ

Great Granny and Pap were fortunate to grow older together. She remained feisty and he, calm and measured.

Grandpa Wheeler's Eyecup

Grandpa was tall and stooped-shouldered when I remember him standing next to little Granny in front of their wishbone mirror dresser as they readied for church. The 'studied' couple made an impression on me—Grandpa's drawn cheeks and small eyes, and Granny's snow-white, soft hair, and small stature.

Their bathroom was off the bedroom. I remember the discovery of granddad's eyecup on the corner shelf. I remember him bending over and showing me how his glass eye went into his eye cavity.

Coats

Mother has bought me coats for the last forty years. It seems I always have been too short on money to afford a big expenditure like a fine quality coat. Some of my coats I lost, like a white nylon hooded jacket trimmed in rabbit fur. I felt terrible. The last coat she bought for me she chose from the local dress shop. I took two home for her to see. She liked the long, plum colored one with black velvet trim inside of the hood.

On my birthday last year my partner wanted to buy me a black faux fur hooded jacket to wear to mother's 90th birthday party. Times had changed and he was providing for me now. Really the long hooded coat from my mother looked better for the occasion but I wore the jacket for his sake.

ಊ

My Hats

I love my hats from many cultures. From childhood when I wanted to go to China I have a gift straw Chinese hat—it is fragile. My straw hats from Hawaii decorate my bedroom door. I bought Dad and me sheepskin hats at a street market in the Northwest. My Vermont hat is similarly fleece-lined, a soft suede leather enlivened by a dark, red, velvet rose on the floppy brim. I still have a purple wool felt cloche which I wore many days in the Northwest, even in the rain. From the gift table at the summer chicken supper in New Hampshire, I bought a summer straw hat with a blue feather.

Dad and I wear my sheepskin gift hats from the Northwest.

My hats are my cultures in between visits to favorite places. My father wore many hats in his many roles. He bought and received hats as gifts. The hall racks would not hold them all.

I bring my hats along in life as reminders of the way I live; I live where I go.

&

My Indian Necklace

Whenever we shopped at the farm store, I would eye the Southwest Native silver jewelry. I found the 'Woman and Bear' with a large green oval for the woman's body. Maybe an egg? Hans surprised me for Christmas with the expensive piece. Usually he bought imitation precious costume jewelry until I had said, "No more. I want the real worth."

Not long after receiving the gift, I brought Tommy cat home from the airport in the middle of the night; I lost the 'Woman and Bear' in the snow when I lifted him out of the car in his carrier. Months later, in the spring, it was found—not on the ground but in Tommy's carrier. The vet found it and sent it home with him on a later visit.

ℰℴ

Dad's Lawn Mowing

I sat on the mowing tractor for the last time—so many memories of Dad on Idler, among the flowering crab, around the Post House, on the ridge above Stagecoach Road. Dad taught me to mow the lane winding down to the gate. He wanted me to be able to take care of the place when he passed on. I moved the garage junk and made way for the tractor to be moved out. When they came for Dad's 'White' tractor, I left before they drove off so that I would not see it taken away.

Dad always said when he could not mow anymore he wanted "to go." I put my hands on the engine cover and blessed it for what it represented to Dad.

At my father's dedication service at the country church, a local farmer friend praised Dad's modesty when he said, "John could have owned any tractor he wanted, but he chose a "White."

After I told the story to my workshop participants, one of the girls gave me a picture of Idler Lane when the trees blossomed in spring. The article honored my father for taking care of the trees.

How perfect that the mower tractor sale, the workshop story, and the picture should sequence the same weekend of his passing several years later.

ଔ

A farmer friend from Campground church said, "John could have had any tractor mower he wanted, but he chose a 'White.'"

The Fish Pond

Today a lady in our storytelling group recalled the importance of a fishpond her father made for her and himself. I recalled my grandmother's house in Woodstock on Park Street. Next to the sidewalk between the back porch and garage. My grandfather had built a stone-lined goldfish pond. I remember the lure of large fish shimmering gold. When I revisited the backyard with my brother sixty-five years later, I could see the disheveled stones somewhat in a circle. How time had destroyed the beauty. The lovely side yard to the house once flanked with pine trees had been filled with new houses.

At a workshop I gave in my Grandmother's hometown, my brother and I returned to the backyard to reminisce. From the place of the falling-down garage, we admired the quaint Victorian back porch and took pictures. Time was one for us.

ॐ

My Chicago cousin-friend and I in Grandpa's side yard showing his proud row of trees.

Joy at Christmas in Grandma's house near Chicago. My sister and oldest Chicago cousin, and Dad's Cousin Marvel, who was like a great aunt. At birthdays and Christmases she sent high interest books for us all. Working in the city she had access to great bookstores. I loved her Chicago accent on the phone. My favorite books were about Miss Muff, who climbed curtains, the Chinese Prince who learned to be his own servant when the family was exiled, and the mysterious appearance of dancing partners for the princesses.

Everyone in the Chicago family looks great in this picture. My father's sister and her husband sit on the left. I adored her outgoing personality. She always "honeyed" me. When I was alone, by choice, becoming my artist self, she called to encourage my pursuits. She was the voice of my artistic family.

Great Grandparents "Granny and Pap", with five great grandchildren.

We usually had to perform for the adults – sing, dance, or recite. My father's family was musical. Both grandmothers sang and played. Grandmother sang at the local opera house. All of the men played musical instruments.

On Dad's Kelsey side is great-grandfather, Reverend J.D. Kelsey, a strong community influence in founding the old people's home and the orphanage. Great Grandpa was Dad's friend through his teen-age years. Dad loved to dance and Granddad always made sure he had the money and car to go dancing in the ballrooms in Chicago. We children knew him by Dad's stories of his friendship and support. As an adult I read his publication, "The Children's Friend." My father carried on the tradition and wanted to be my friend. He always was present and supportive on the worst occasions of my life from youth to middle age. There was little he did not know about me. I was loyal to my father's trust in me until the end of the family.

The Doll

I remember asking my mother for a beautiful doll. Grandma Kelsey had made me a black, velvet-stuffed seal—not the same as a doll even though I cuddled it.

Years later, my neighbor ran to the front porch to give me her gift in between packing to move. She wanted to give me something for taking care of her flowers.

She did not know what else to give me; only this one doll remained who did not have a home in her lovely doll collection. This doll was an outsider—an orphan who did not have a home. My friend had told the doll that I had no children and that I would take excellent care of her.

It was interesting to receive her, because I had felt like an orphan as a child. I named her "Blessing" and realized the importance of receiving her to complete my Vermont home. With my friend moving I, too, had to realize my completeness.

ଓ

The Mystic Topaz

I had spent a flat six weeks in Australia and New Zealand even though the trip went well. Life events seemed normal rather than paranormal. Perhaps because I manifest at a high level much of the time and the days were normal I did not notice much unusualness. Also, I was tired emotionally—unable to respond too well.

Finally, my trip turned metaphysical. I started in Honolulu visiting Tiffany's. Then at the end of the trip, I revisited Tiffany's to see the same beautiful ring, a Mandarin garnet. In Vermont after the trip when looking over the fine jewelry at Penney's, to my surprise, a beautiful ring like the garnet at Tiffany's fascinated me. The color appealed because of its blue tint and subdued orange. The name captured me, "Mystic Topaz." I confirmed my birthright to a wealthy life with the purchase of my birthstone, the topaz.

ౙ

Lost Rings

The last time I visited my Vermont home, I completed the décor with new light fixtures, pictures on the walls, hall and bedroom, and also new furniture and floor coverings from far away places from my neighbor who was moving.

I put my prosperity rings in a small container and commented that it was a strange holder. When I left, I could not find my jade ring or my Mystic Topaz anywhere.

All of my treasure is together, hiding, waiting for me to discover it.

ౙ

Passion

The most beautiful gift arrived from Cold Water Creek, from mother in time for my birthday. She sent a detailed note of descriptions. I could tell she was working hard to keep track of everything, (the red velvet top shimmered over the long skirt). She had included the cut-along description—entitled "passion." Mother always expressed her love of beauty in clothes and jewelry but never had her message included the idea of passion. Her love of beauty was passionate.

₧

The Tangible Substance of God

Most of my talismans come from someone else. I love and reflect our family's value of beauty in common-life art as well as in music and art and fine furnishings.

However, my own medicine bag made of beaver fur came from a Northwest powwow Native American artist. A bone closure with an antique flowered trader's bead secures the loop. Although I do not tell the bag's contents or look at the talismans because they are secret, I know their symbolic power in my life to represent what I value and what I want to have in my life

The recounting of description and source, function, relationship, and meaning of a talisman make up a story. When the account is retold more than one time to more than two people it becomes traditional in our repertoire of story. The story reflects our values and beliefs. The body of stories, our life stories, becomes a resource to us for knowing who we are and represents the tangible means of preserving ourselves. Others can know us deeply through our values, when we no longer can tell our story. Others can pass on stories verbally, or if we have written our accounting, or shown it with artifacts, we will have lassoed the tangible substance of ourselves and God within us.

Celebrating Birthdays

When my father was nearing ninety, he called me and did not tell me the story, as he usually did, about driving from Chicago to St. Louis the night I was born. Maybe it was not on my birthday. Certainly it was not his memory failing; but I told him the story and followed it with a light-hearted comment that he did not know what he was getting into. He responded with a dear thought that he knew he had a lot to look forward to.

ઠ૦

My father's 90th birthday, September 1910-April 2001. A celebration included dinner at a country log cabin, country music, and dancing for many friends from all walks of life. I commemorated him as a "Lamp Unto My Feet" and talked about his love of collecting lamps.

CHAPTER IV

Confirmation

"Like being on top of a topographical map, distance was minimal with complete balance on a pinnacle, protected by the calm air—I was one with God's omnipresence."

Crossing the meadow on the climb up Mount Rainier.

CHAPTER IV

Confirmation

Paradise Climb

Excerpted from *Dancing up the Mountain,*
A Guide to Writing Your Life Story,
Jacqueline K. Kelsey, PhD,1999

Paradise Inn

Do I dare stay overnight at the Paradise Inn when I do not have enough in the checking account to pay for it? It would be ten o'clock after attending the lecture. How could I possibly drive four hours back to my suburban home when I was tired? "There's one room left. You're in luck," the desk clerk said. He showed me the room, number nine, off the lounge, small. "I'll have to think about it," I stalled. Looking into the dining room I speculated on how it would feel to wake up in the morning. In addition, I would have dinner and I would be able to stay for the program.

The porters invited guests and the public to hear the doctor from the Tibetan expedition. The Tibetans who attended the team would answer questions after the slides. This was a serendipitous event because I had returned from my climb to Glacier-Lookout that afternoon.

The whole evening was adding up for me at the Paradise Inn. How could I have known earlier at the coffee shop that my finding directions to enter the park at the "Paradise Entrance" would unfold to give me my final gift before leaving home for the last six years?

୧୬

The Climb

Climbing the mountain as far as I could, I saw where the glacier gouged the side of the mountain. It pictured my life, "I had remained unscathed," I mused. At my destination I panned the miles of summits from the glacial outlook peak. A song from my youth voiced itself through me as I listened to myself singing quietly "On Christ the solid rock I stand… ."

Exhausted from my preparation to move back to the Midwest, I had only twenty-four hours left to regroup. Also, the spiritual teaching I had subjected myself to from my mentor all week had left me weary. I felt the trauma of recent lost love as well. Needing to rest, I easily gave in to being one with God at the summit; my loss and the glacier-gouged mountain were history—ancient destruction in time and insignificant compared to infinity and forever. I had been spared; the destruction was pictured for me rather than my having had to take it into myself.

Absolved by infinitude, I stayed at the top long enough to be alone with the peaks for as far as I could see. The air was still and quiet. The air view seemed familiar—all was close at hand. *Like being on top of a topographical map, distance was minimal with complete balance on a pinnacle, protected by the calm air—I was one with God's omnipresence.*

When I returned to join the other climbers on the path, I was with company. A young couple said they, too, had needed this getaway for an uplift. We walked down the path together, laughing and chatting all the way, a celebration return to Paradise Inn.

ℬ

Guided Climb

Although I was alone on the trek up the mountain, I was assisted. Two older women guides, who volunteered to help climbers, suggested that I could cut across the meadow to Dead Horse Creek and get a great view of the top. My breath was too short to climb straight ahead and up the path. I would at least see the white cap because I thought I could not make it to the top. I lay on the bench near the bridge and rested in the view from the meadow filled with flowers. I could see the snowy bright top of the mountain. When "she was out" I had awed at her through the rhododendrons from the edge of my yard on the lake, two hundred miles away.

After I had rested for fifteen minutes on the bridge over Dead Horse Creek, a young man who had come down from the top hiked near me. He said I was sure I would make it because the path from Dead Horse Creek inclined at an angle. We chatted for several minutes about life; we "philosophized," as my guide friend at the coffee shop would say.

ℬ

Evening Focus

Today, philosophizing seemed connected—it came from the soul. Inspired by "her" glowing iridescence under the sun, the white glaze pouring down her sides like icing, I walked by myself slowly and steadily to the first lookout. I determined to make it with rest to the second lookout—higher up—Glacier-Lookout. I heard the quiet surrounding me and saw forever; spanning the distant north and south—the undisturbed, peaks of rock simultaneously pointing toward the sky. Unafraid, I was surprised to have come upon a privileged view without "disturbing" it or "impacting" it. I was close to bare mountain, a monument to God.

My climb this day was symbolic of six years of rigorous preparation, stages of personal and spiritual growth, care of the body through massage, dance, and physical therapy and, finally, arrival at the top. Hearing and seeing the preparation of the expedition in order to climb the Tibetan mountain pictured in detail my healthy climb today, to imprint a new and better future for myself, peaked by mountain top perspectives.

&

The Evening Replay

Returning to Paradise Lodge, I had to make my choice. Another couple had asked for the room after I did, and when I reappeared, I quickly said I would take it, if it were agreeable with them. I needed to stay over and it was the last room. Their appearance and wait seemed to be a challenge and confirmation of my willingness to play out the scenario completely. They were disappointed but very pleasant. After dinner, the lounge filled with listeners for the talk and slide show.

How fortuitous that I would hear about the long preparation to earn money for the expedition, the special care at each of the stations before striking out for a higher level, the Tibetan's tea service—a greeting for the climbers when they would arrive at a new station. With all of their modern communication and technology, their uppermost concern and focus was personal care of themselves at each level and preparation for the next station at a yet higher altitude. The doctor emphasized that without the body there would be no climb.

The doctor's last slide and commentary ironically stressed how the pinnacle, when finally reached, provided a space the size of a kitchen tabletop. The climb—the challenge and the demand, the personal accomplishment and teamwork—made the two-year preparation for supplies, the fundraising, and the rigorous trek worthwhile.

ॐ

Morning View

The next morning, sun streamed through my small window after a solitary night in my single bed in the room on the hall close to the office. Because I had no change of clothes or overnight care items, there was no fussing; I could hurry to the lobby and return to the world.

The waiters seated me at table number nine, my room number. It was the only one available because I had asked for a table with a view of the mountain. Tucked away in a cozy corner under an eave, I was the first one to be seated for breakfast. How uncomplicated, alone and fresh life seemed at six-thirty in the morning. After yesterday's climb and life's replay through the slide show, the strong message of self-care from the doctor had impressed me. What if I had not stayed over? What if I had pushed too hard? The dining room was quiet and the lounge empty. The rich coffee invigorated me to hurry outdoors.

After breakfast, I hurried to the parking lot at seven o'clock. There was no activity; no one was around. Unexpectedly, a young man suddenly ran out from behind his car shouting, "Did you see her?" He was waving his camera, shouting while he came closer to get into his car to leave. "She went that way, a beautiful red fox; I tried to get her picture." He shut his car door and drove away.

In the silence, I opened my car door and thought, "I am here. No, I did not see her." She had visited, preceded me, and left her talisman message with no picture available. The medicine wheel's child of the South spoke: "I am a foxy lady to have climbed the metaphorical mountain for six years and to have lived to tell the story—to return to my world, unscathed having created my own slide show."

ॐ

Table Top Reflection

I wondered if I had chosen the confirmation climb to show myself what I had been aspiring to and desiring. The steps and meandering below the top, over a six-year period, were not always linear, perhaps "as crooked as a dog's hind leg." I lost my way a few times but my heart prevailed.

The day before climbing, I had listened to my friend's direction at the coffee shop—"Be sure to drive in the park at the Paradise Entrance." The eventuating "table top" experience gave me the view of all that had been and would be; it provided me with a place of perspective to see that I had arrived at the top and showed me by other climbers' example that I had done it by caring for myself and having faith in God.

Today, fifteen years later, I have had to wait years before seeing from the top again. I had heard and seen quiet and undisturbed mountaintops in the distance forever, unchanging. Mount Aspiration in New Zealand was a future hoped-for, a withheld icon for travel, around the world to Bangkok, Hong Kong, Singapore, and French Polynesia whether literally or in Spirit or in some other form.

৪৩

CHAPTER V

Soul Space

"Under the dormer eaves a long closet housed my child-size furniture. It was my own space….When I created the "Apple Shed" and spent so much time there without opening a business, a grade school classmate asked me if I were playing house…."

A reminder of lace curtains from the birthing room in our Vermont home.

CHAPTER V

Soul Space

Create Homes

Concentration

Time is one among my tangibles because ironically it reflects the intangible quality of love I experience with my forbearers. Similarly, I am one with myself no matter where I am and in that space, I am present with no sense of time. All places share the same environment, therefore, the same space. Being at home in more than one place, in many places—even needing to spread among many, is the way the soul expands itself, I have been told, according to Plato's idea of the soul's expression. Therefore, I have many homes going at one time—Vermont, the Northwest, the Midwest and my ongoing transmigration including going to the North Pacific Ocean and making it part of my Northwest triangle. My final flight to the South Pacific completes my dream.

Because I have concentrated, I must go deeper. The idea came to me from a teaching nun in Boston at a conference on transcendentalism, a favorite literary theme in my 19th-Century American literature studies. She presented the idea that the deeper the descent, the more one ascends—transcending, all living is possible when one descends deeper in thinking. I have expanded many small spaces to be large enough for a temporary home—like a hospital bed with all my purse contents spread in front of me to equip "my house."

Having the "high watch" over all places at the same time, I feel like the eagle. Conversely, could the eagle's fishing expertise partly be due to his high, wide perspective, enabling him to zero in on the small space of the fish he seeks? What I have known to be true all of my life, being in small environs, I sometimes have failed to put my experience into a larger perspective. Gardening, singing, dancing, portraying life activate my soul's attributes so that I can fly. Over time my creative life becomes my flight pattern.

Physically expanding people's spaces and activity to fill a large space is desirable. Because of appreciating living in the confines of a small area, I used the Post House and Apple Shed to expand to a larger context in teaching through workshops, publishing, and developing radio programs.

I risked experimenting at a workshop for six people, held on the entire floor of a library. We spread the energy of our work and persons to fill floor space areas, stacks of books, and aisles beneath the windows. Similarly, I have experienced expansion of space with houses on land, those atop amorphous waters bounded by land, ones in the limitless air and sky with flight to the faraway above this world. All kinds of space make up the comfort zone of my homes.

My soul requires them all, sequentially and simultaneously, to create magic, like the disappearing hut of the Hawaiian magic show. A transcendent mind/soul can create the faith necessary for "seeing is believing and believing is seeing." That which appears in the environment like hearts, flowers, and feathers, can be experienced with their accompanying soul attributes of love, freedom, and grace.

Skeleton of the aviary. There was enough room for one long room and a hallway inside the aviary. I imagine with romantic thoughts the cedar grove- peacocks waltzing among the trees. Our corn stalk tepee centered in the cedars next to the aviary.

Corn Teepee

On the south hill of the farm posed the shake-shingled aviary, a get-away within the grove of cedar trees.

My adventurous friend would go to the farm with me and walk the rows of stalks to pick up leftover corn. The goal was to get treats for our family's horses.

One time we ventured down through the field, to the railroad tracks below, to look for Indian beads. I found a grooved rock cylinder and thought it was a cylindrical Indian bead.

Another time we gathered corn stalks and ears and dragged them up the hill to make a cornstalk teepee amidst the cedars. The teepee was big enough to sit in. What fun! We left it up for weeks.

છ

My House in a Hospital Bed

The nurse insisted that I be taken to the hospital. I was part of a visiting school team and started having stress attacks in my chest; it was near the finish of my dissertation. The doctor kept me in the hospital four days for testing. My colleagues left to return home to the university and I was stuck in the Chicago suburbs. I did not tell my parents because they were headed on an overseas trip of a lifetime.

When my sister and brother-in-law came to the hospital, I explained my stress story while emptying my purse contents on the bed. I had been trying to make order with my possessions. Typically I have taken a few things to create a tiny home in which to survive, be happy, and thrive. Fortunately I did not have a heart problem. I have lived "a charmed life."

છ

The Swedish House

I quit my job, took my folklore course on an independent basis and joined my husband for a new job in Rockford. I was determined not to be left behind. We rented a miniature farmhouse on the back lot of a house in the Swedish section of town. We created a storybook house by renovating the basement and its bathroom. My whole family came to visit us and slept on the patchwork carpet upstairs. The kids loved looking down through the antique grate floor register into the living room below. When our son worked on his first engineering internship, he lived in the basement.

ॐ

Mother-In-Law's Loft

When I prepared to move to the Northwest from Illinois, I advertised for a sunny apartment on the water—"A Teacher, NO parties."

Seven people called me in Illinois about their available apartments. When my sister and her husband drove with me to the Northwest, we stayed in one of the potential rentals. It needed a lot of work. The other apartment situated on the water, sported a loft with a pitched roof, move-in ready.

I created a bedroom under the north eave. The space opened into a small living room at the open end of the eave where the ceiling allowed enough height to stand.

A kitchen and eating room and sitting area made up the other half of the A-frame on the waterside. A playroom with pretend furniture filled the eave over the stairwell.

The house grew when the landlord built a deck and I grew a container garden out my kitchen door, overlooking the lake, a reserve for me to grow in for several years.

ॐ

The Keyesport Cabin

Getting away—a home for a week—a safe one! The owner turned out to be a nurse at the home where my mother stayed. All my needs were met—privacy and near the water. To these basics I added luxurious pansies for the front deck porch, "Ski" soft drinks, fresh fruit, animal crackers, and tea. I made a bouquet of dried sweet peas and gathered pinecones from the park area. Every night my life came to order. No work, no responsibility, only caring for me. I placed creams and lotions near me and used them regularly. I took walks and rides, ate in all the local spots, made a doctor's appointment, visited the chiropractor and bought myself a birthday gift for the upcoming celebration at my Sunday workshop. I even went to Bible study at the local Methodist church.

જી

The bottom of the water tower still stands. We call it the Post House because it is now on Stagecoach Road.

The metal tank crumples on the ground where the tower originally stood. Seven cisterns on the farm provided water and filled the large tank.

The Post House

A tiny house on the prairie, a make-believe, two-story house made from the old water tower base. Upstairs a bed, desk, book shelf and dresser; downstairs a window seat, kitchen area, work area, and floor to ceiling shelves displaying serving dishes, candleholders, floral displays and home memorabilia. It looked as if I could live there. I equipped large plastic storage boxes with bedding and clothes. The red metal cabinet from my first husband's grandmother was stacked with my games, eating and cooking utensils, cups, glasses, and pans. We moved in a mini-refrigerator and baking oven.

Each season I cleaned the place as if I were living there. I hung small Christmas lights in the window and wound a strand around the banister. Dad allowed me to put in new wiring for safety and a better look. He fertilized outdoor plantings and regularly sprayed the weeds on the brick patio. Dad hardly ever drank a Coke from the cabin refrigerator when he had been mowing but he came in to cool off.

We planned to expand into a new room, over the brick patio, with a view over the east field. When we talked about winterizing the post house, adding a room and running water—Dad cried out, "but I won't be here." He always mowed around the building and the green metal shed. The Post House was his playhouse too. At night, near Thanksgiving, the family, including grandchildren, trekked from the house on the hill to the 1820 water tower. Forming a snake line, we carried our thermoses of hot chocolate.

By candlelight Mother told stories of her childhood, the farm and, the pioneers who settled the farm in the 1820's. My brother made a video of us gathered in the small circle listening to Mother.

ॐ

1920-2011 Gateway Farm, named by Grandmother Andrews in the 1960's.

My Parents' Home

I am better now but for a while I could hardly enjoy living in my mother's home knowing how much she would like to be at home and how much she depended on me to get her there. It seemed unfair that she should have to sit at the nursing home watching TV rather than relaxing at home. Everything belonged to her and nothing seemed available to her. She learned to enjoy new activities and people but never gave up her love of home place.

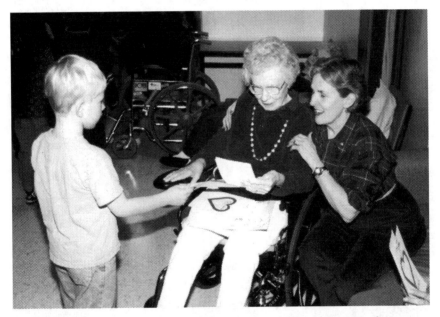

My Mother receives a valentine from a visiting child at the nursing home.

I have wondered about life's turnabouts. My parents worked their whole lives to build a farm home—"their destiny" my mother said—and now they were not able to enjoy its comfort in their final years—like a living death!—not unlike my father's leaving his home never to return when he went to a big city hospital.

☙

Our Mobile Home

Mother and I ate Kentucky Fried Chicken tonight in the parking lot at the grocery store. Her Grand Marquis was our mobile home because I could not transport her from the wheel chair out of the car into the house. She did not want to go home again and eat in the driveway or in the field. We had ice cream drumsticks for dessert and afterwards came home to get the quilts so that she could choose which one should be entered in the show Friday. She agreed on the red and white quilt. "Tommy" cat joined us on her lap for a ride back to the nursing home.

&

Play House

Tonight, sitting by the wood stove on a rainy night, I tried to entertain myself by reading *Simple Abundance—A Day Book of Comfort and Joy* by Sarah Ban Breathnach. I moved ahead to July and chose an entry on the hobby of taking care of one's home, creating a home ongoing and forever. That is what I love to do.

When I was a child, I practiced this skill; it was my hobby then. Under the eaves across the front of the house in my home town, I created my world out of children's furniture and my dolls. Because I took such good care of it, when a neighborhood child wanted to play in it, my mother turned her down because I had just finished cleaning and straightening up. My mother wanted me to know that she supported me when she tells the story.

As an adult I have a birthing room in the Victorian house on River Street out East. The room reminds me of my house under the eaves. Recently, my neighbor friend added a wallpaper border of large grey, pink, and blue hydrangea to cover the tattered edges of the original paper.

The Birthing Room

Our farm cat from the Midwest, Thomas Aquinas, sunned on a down feather pillow from Germany, gathering strength for his last months of retired life. French lace curtains draped inside the floral curtains.

I restored the former closet formerly filled with unused furniture, to its birthing room status for my get-away, dream-nap sessions. Children's books and stuffed bears kept me company while I disappeared into my child's mind and shut the door to the master bedroom.

The blooming crabapple tree boughs draped over the roof and snowed down petals in such great profusion that neighbors came to take pictures.

On a quiet afternoon when the window opened to the river, the gurgles quieted my mind. In this springtime, I wrote my stories about the animals that came to visit beneath the tall black door on our front porch.

ലാ

The birthing room is the room at the top of the roof peak off the master bedroom.

My Own Home

Under the dormer eaves a long closet housed my child-size furniture. It was my own space.... When I created the "Apple Shed" and spent so much time there without opening a business, a grade school classmate asked me if I were playing house... Although when I was a kid I took my housekeeping seriously, it was not as much fun as creating a home and story center from the old service garage where Grandpa stored his bumper crops of apples.

I appreciated the classmate's sympathetic view of the fun I was having, especially because it was the only house I owned by myself at the time. I felt I had been given permission to play again.

໖

Cedar tree artwork on the East end of the Apple
Shed is my reminder of the farm grove.

The Apple Shed

My sister called to say she had received bids on the old gray garage service building at the factory. I wanted to buy it and use the rent income from it to pay expenses on the house. After getting into the deal, I realized the lot behind the cement block building brought in no income, a loss of several hundred per month in my plan.

Ah well, sentiment prevailed. I would own a piece of the old glove factory, my Grandfather Andrews' business. Gradually, I fixed one of the roofs and the drainpipes. Hans painted the cement block building and I painted folk art nature scenes on the east side.

A dream come true—I had spoken the Jabez prayer and two days later I was headed toward ownership of a building in which I could create a story center. An inner sanctum in the center gazebo would be my writing center.

℘

Find Home

Delight in life has come from choosing a safe, small space to wrap myself in with a few select necessities for my creative spirit. Because I live where I go, my reduced house of life helps me toward rebirth; otherwise my plate would be too full for me to concentrate and fly.

In Hawaii, filling my car with vases of flowers from the Hawaii market and distilling the perfume as I drove, enabled me to heal lost love with beauty. Surveying the symbolic contents of my life purse in a hospital room bed enabled me to surround and squeeze out of life what I needed to revive and continue in my academic challenge to finish research. Sometimes the lesson has been bigger. I spent the last week after a flight to Hawaii and New Zealand holding up in a motel room in the entertainment capitol of the world in order to focus my travel in the world on connecting with world culture rather than entertainment. I needed to emerge from the South Pacific atmosphere after hibernation, with a new creative direction in my life.

Recently I have been terrified by the awareness that I am homeless. Is this true soul space? In the Northwest I used to doubt that I would come out on top and feared becoming a bag lady. The reality was great enough that I turned down an extra role for a bag lady. Recently I had the same feelings of having nowhere to go, no sacred space to call my own, even temporarily. I had grown into physically and spiritually larger spaces and yet they were not homes. Could I return to a closet or would I create a larger new home? Perhaps I was not able to be without a tangible home?

The recent transition period was marked by the auction of our century old farm and its fifty-year-old family home and the loss of our historic Vermont home due to a mudslide.

The consequential move to a New York style basement apartment, under a florist's shop in a three-storied historic site building, was chosen in order to take a temporary, part-time teaching job at a nearby university.

The security of ownership where I could live is located in the Midwest where there is no work, yet. The Apple Shed provides a daytime resting place, literally, in the bed of my Grandfather who built the glove factory for which the Apple Shed was a service building and storage space for his apples from the farm orchard. Temporarily, I returned to sleeping in a friend's home.

Have I already increased the soul's space with my barn over-flowing? Certainly it seems so with all of my increased wealth. It seems so with my new book, *Beneath the Tall Black Door* and *Flight Beyond the Stars,* on its way to publication in the spring. In midwinter my mind-plan expanded the travel to the East—Hong Kong, Singapore, Bangkok, and Bora Bora to continue the trip to Australia and New Zealand I had begun several years ago. In the past when I needed to move on, I took time out to climb higher and see where I had been and where I was going. The Apple Shed has been the source and storehouse of my creative thinking and prosperity but where will I live?

Am I destined to be in the air? I have been teaching with great effects on my students' spiritual lives as they integrate myth and story. In a sense I have experienced practice flight before my unknown next step. I will pack my bag with talismans. I continue the zigzag climb to get perspective and grounding simultaneously as I did twenty years ago at Mt. Rainier. I am one with my life. Do I simply need to go deeper? What would that look like? How? Or do I need to wait? It seems like the balloon strings have been cut. As I accept "no home," I expect my soul to find its own moon; I am my home knowing that the true self takes me deeper and higher. As in the story of Daedalus, the admonition is not to go too near the sun. During the Advent season, I am asking what I am waiting for. I am ready to receive the gift. Yesterday I heard a reminder about gifts: The Divine gift is always greatly bestowed.

A Summary of House Plans (Soul's Home) Over Twenty Years

Leaving a Midwest home at midlife; starting over in a loft overlooking a lake in the Northwest.

Recreating life from within; healing my spiritual vacuum.

Creating workshops on life story.

Refurbishing a second home in Vermont and moving back to the Midwest; helping take care of my parents' home.

Becoming "a child of the wind," as my mother said I should be.

Writing my first book.

Leaving home because the farm sold; fixing up the Apple Shed, a place of prosperity.

Losing a home to a mudslide in Vermont; fixing up an apartment in Vermont for temporary living.

Experiencing homelessness again and losing my faith "to fly;" A groundless groundling.

Starting over by continuing my second book, *Flight Beyond the Stars.*

Starting over in the Apple Shed, home and work place by day.

Finding an unconventional home in a single bed for sleeping at night with only a few possessions/talismans, like my Beaver "medicine bag."

As in the hospital bed, home alone, I spiral upward. Being content spiritually at home, while my barn overflows.

Marketing my first book and publishing the second book; I have a future.

Charting the long distance flight.

Flying unfettered into a world home, like Internet worldwide radio.

Finding my spiritual teaching role after twenty-five years of preparation.

Guide to Wholeness and Creativity

What has helped me come to myself and to God?

- The natural environment—the tangible substance of God. Water, eagles, hawks, and heron—rebirth through flight

- Self Expression through the arts—beauty

- Perspective on daily life as a common-life art experience

- Dreams—knowing the spiritual side of myself to make the long distance flight—

- Feeling heart and following the "Desires of my Heart"

- Consistently using the same elements in perspective and content over time

- Being willing to fly in the dark

CHAPTER VI

Flight—The Dream of Flying Higher

"The sermon for the day was 'Journey to the Unfamiliar with Faith.' Certainly I had come to the Outback with the expectation of moving my life forward;.."

Going higher requires going deeper to find the water beneath me, just as the Scripture taught the woman in the desert.

When my parents built their home on the hill, two lakes would not hold water so they "witched" a well near the house. The well never went dry.

CHAPTER VI

Flight—The Dream of Flying Higher

South Pacific Take Off

Going to the South Pacific had probably been a dream since childhood when I lay on the rug next to the radio listening to Mary Martin and Ezio Pinza's album of the musical, "South Pacific." On my way to New Zealand via a direct flight from Honolulu, I stopped over for four days. The "Red Shoes" experience recounts part of the preliminary steps.

For fifteen years I had been saying, "I am going to the South Pacific." Thus, five years earlier than takeoff I bought a guidebook at Borders in Chicago on the "Magnificent Mile," to envision myself going alone. Transportation on the islands, disease, and cultural bias made many islands unappealing. Therefore, I made a step toward Australia and New Zealand when I shared my dream with a psychic on the Big Island. Her visions of places and what I would receive encouraged me to go. She gave me place names where I could expect to receive something special for myself.

When I arrived in Auckland, the New Zealand air agent held me for three days, planning the particulars for travel in New Zealand and Australia. Six weeks was a long time for me to plan in detail and to commit to on the heels of my fourteen-hour flight. It was work to coordinate flights. Ironically and significantly during the six weeks I would spend a great deal of time in the air because of the distances between the Honolulu and Auckland, Sydney and Alice Springs in the Outback, and the South Island of New Zealand.

Each day in Auckland I spent the morning drinking "flat whites," tidying up daily life and learning where to go and how to get along. Afternoons, I explored on long walks, visiting museums, and island hopped by ferry. I planned an overnight two-day trip to rural, sheep-herding New Zealand

After three days at the boutique hotel I had no plans for where to go. I recalled a guidebook description of an island and headed out. Not finding a bed-and-breakfast open by walking the territory with my guidebook, I went to a bookstore in a neighborhood where I experienced, serendipitously, a refined Bed-and-Breakfast. My trip had begun. I rested with heated towels, a flower garden view at breakfast and a lavender silk sachet for my pillow, to give me peace.

New Red Sandals
You Are Beautiful
Ponsonby
Mount Victoria
Compensation-Places
No Time
The Dry Pools
The Days Run Together

New Red Sandals

All following stories excerpted *Mystic
Topaz, A Tale from Down Under*
Jacqueline Kelsey, 1996

A five hour difference between Honolulu and the Midwest and so today again I was up at 4:30 a.m., walking down to the lobby and out onto the street after my evening of seclusion in the hotel. Sporting a new pedicure, my pretty feet matched the magenta red and pinks of my new Hawaiian flowing slacks and hibiscus design shirt which I bought last February on the Big Island. I chose my new red sandals to start the week.

"For the Birds," street fun in Honolulu.

The front desk was quiet; the soft spoken, dark-skinned man directed me to fresh coffee at the convenience store across the street. Before greeting the outer world, I savored my Hawaiian environment by focusing on the artifacts and decor in the hotel lobby. Behind the lobby the koi pond flanked tiers of lavender orchids. The back hallway, leading to the elevators, archived photos of the taro plots where the Royal Hawaiian Hotel now stands. I am sure most people did not take the time to notice the portrait of the Prince because it was in the back hallway. The hotel seemed ordinary with its orchids and fishpond. However, when I read the plaque I learned that I was on former royal land.

Across the street, six police cars parked in several directions as if they were surrounding the store. The deskman reassured me that they parked there to get their morning coffee. "There are lots of police cars available in Honolulu." I, too, got my coffee-to-go and sauntered in the dark over to the park bench across the street. The water jet spray motioned the grass slowly into the heat of the day, while the stoic statue of King David Kalakaua presided over the sunrise.

With the slowness of the sunrise, I practiced watching and seeing: the darkening to light sky, the increasing traffic, the breakfast outdoor veranda opening to customers, the hotel lobbies filling with overnight guests. I awoke to my awe of being in Hawaii. Too early to walk to the Royal Hawaiian Shopping Center on Waikiki, I ate breakfast at the Thai veranda across the street. I needed to let the day in slowly and therefore, returned to my hotel room to rest. I read about the Queen and her music and about the island of Molokai.

At lunchtime I walked in "my red sandals" to the edge of the terrace dining room; the ocean swept me into the blue with balmy trade winds. Marion, my server, shared her life with me. She had told herself that if she did not make it into medical school she would go around the world. Indeed, after her trip she worked serving people in order to live in Hawaii. For thirty-five years she had been serving people. Watching the waves I disappeared into the realm of imagining beyond my sojourn to the place where no destination or desire dares.

℥

You Are Beautiful

"My mother says you are beautiful," spoke the Korean girl. All of us in the mineral waters laughed and played. The only American, I swam with my new Korean friends. I had walked with some of the girls through the woods the night before to see the glowworms on the rocks after the Maori dinner. The mother's words jolted me because I had been feeling fat and pudgy since I gained weight on the trip. In daylight, I recognized the girl who had helped me walk the difficult path the night before.

After the spa swim, we gathered in the lobby to catch our buses. They made me a center of taking pictures and we exchanged addresses. The girls' last picture included the one girl who took pictures because everyone had wanted one with me. Finally, we stood together. All of us ladies were teachers.

At breakfast I had joined a table of women from Taiwan. I was among friends of the world.

છ

Ponsonby

The zoo and Ponsonby—two destinations I was determined to reach. At the end of the planning day with Miriam at the airline office, I decided there was enough time and energy for a new activity. Taking the bus, the right one on the right side of the street, and a return at night was a test. The nearest rider, a medical recruiter, asked me to sit with her—attractive, single, with a social life entertaining friends at home—she liked to cook. She told me about the red light district, slum area, renovation, and the long road of restaurants which led to the Heme Bay below.

I walked the boulevard length of the restaurants. The second story Thai restaurant by the Samoan church piqued my interest on the return walk. It would be close to transportation after dinner. Also, I had decided to eat early and pay less for a $30—$40 dinner. The Thai large shrimp in peanut sauce plumped down next to a small heap of shredded cabbage, garnished with carrot leaves and rosettes. For dessert, I delighted in banana fritters and ice cream presented among sliced fruits. Between courses jasmine ethers effused from a rolled warm cloth presented on a stemmed bowl which matched the blue and white leaf plates used for presenting my banana dessert.

At dusk, I caught the right bus and lumbered back to the hill of the city where the Auckland City tower beamed out. From the backside of the city I could see the tall city buildings and find my way to Queens Street and the hotel not far from the ferry dock. I was beginning to circle my way around Auckland.

ॐ

Mount Victoria

"You can get to the grave of the Maori Chief off Kerr Street." I stepped over the road chain and ambled down the grassy roadbed, passed the roofs of houses below before coming to the churchyard cemetery. The first large iron-fenced grave which I could see from the grassy roadbed did not belong to Eru Patone, although the cemetery seemed like a fitting place. Clumps of orange iris grew wild alongside the grassy roadbed. Soon it became clear that I was gaining height while I circumvented the mountain.

In the distance around the bend, I saw a large man. Fear grew as I kept walking because I would not be able to get away if I needed to. I could only go forward toward him. I decided to walk toward him. A large friendly dog greeted me. The large man turned out to be a large pregnant woman whose T-shirt was smeared with mud stains. "It's a bit of a climb," she said breathily. I knew I could make it if she had.

My foot slipped on the muddy path at the top and I was down on my knee. The embattlement structure looked like an abandoned "no-enter area." I followed the pregnant woman's instructions and warily crept down the steep path behind the elementary school where the children played during outside recess. I was on the same street as the bed-and-breakfast but several blocks around the bend on the watersidewalk.

The place named Takaranga, given by the healer, admonished me to seek out this place in New Zealand. By chance I learned about the mountain after I arrived; however, I was wondering if it were the same place. The mountain where the Chief of Peace had spent time had allowed me to take a faith walk before starting my climb of healing during the following five weeks. I rested overnight in the neighborhood below the mountain.

There was still my quest to find the Maori chief's grave.

ॐ

Compensation-Places

Even though I was not able to see all I desired, I was filled with New Zealand. Seeing the brochure on the West Coast presented by the ladies at the tourist center in Devonport, thinking about the tour around the West part of the city bus, going by ferry to Waiwera to enjoy the baths all came to me serendipitously, not as tourist information but as a personal exchange. Someone wanted to help me—to give to me. I experienced the places as if I had been there, even though the time and circumstances prevented me from an actual experience. I felt complete.

In Australia even though I did not take city tours and long tourist ferry rides, I was satisfying myself with the introduction to places. It seemed enough.

- The taxi ride home from the play and seeing harbor lights and the historic Russell Hotel,

- The ferry ride to Manly instead of a tourist 2½ hour harbor cruise.

- The tour to the Blue Mountains including downtown Sydney and the ferry ride which included a harbor cruise after, seeing the Olympic grounds at night, instead of independent tours of each.

- The artistic rendition of bats in the museum instead of bats in the preserve; there was not time to get around to all of the exhibits.

ॐ

No Time

Due to planning with the agent, I missed the opportunities to enjoy a trip to the West Black Beach. No time between 12:25 and my return to pick up tickets. It had been my last opportunity for a getaway. Was this related to having money and not being able to get at it because of the limit on my credit card? Because there was no time to fit in a visit, I had to enjoy both water environments in my mind. Strange that I would be restrained from water before going to Sydney and a trip to the desert. I would experience more water and beach outside of Sydney. Yes, there would be water spas on the South Island in the weeks ahead. I would have to wait. What I wanted did come at a different time. Perhaps the best of my trip was not to begin until Australia and the South Island of New Zealand and finally to finish on Molokai?

On the ferry to Devonport I met a university professor in applied linguistics. She told me about the popularity of digital story and I told her about "living in story." We planned to have coffee on my return to Auckland at the end of my trip. In looking back there was no time to meet on the evening of my return or before early morning take off. We talked on the phone and it seemed her interest in my life story work had waned when she researched how many Australian resources there were for the work.

ଷ

The Dry Pools

Again, all day I spent time getting ready to leave—laundry, hotel arrangements, and two visits to Air New Zealand. Midday, the agent learned there were no "Red Kangaroo" seats left on the Ghan—only one seat left—a Red Kangaroo "shared sleeper" for

$500.00. We re-routed, arranging two days extra in Sydney for only $58.00. I arranged a flight from Sydney to Alice Springs instead even though I had wanted to cover ground across the desert in luxury of the train. The experience of getting there was part of my sojourn into the outback and into my interior. Another loss—the hotel chain's "hot deal" arrangement would cost three times the amount of my boutique hotel in Auckland. The third day, the debit card exceeded the daily limit at the Sydney Hotel.

For rest I looked forward to a coastal bus ride ending at Waiwera Spa spring pools. After the spa experience in Rotorura being cut short so that I could go to the Buried Village, I was determined to visit this important Maori spring spa.

After a ferry ride in the dark, I bussed up to Devonport and switched busses to the City of Takapuna. I had not been able to get away from trip packing and preparation until 8:00 p.m. There was no help at the bus stops other than the posted "Hibiscus" bus. The Japanese driver for another line said he did not think there was any way to get all the way to Waiwera. After an hour in the late evening, I decided to re-route and return to Devonport. No coast to see, in the dark, no pools to relax in and "no more ferries," said my Maori bus driver. I was alone. She wanted me to stay on the bus until the next ferry arrived; she said it was the last one. I read her family invitation to a relative's wedding on the West coast and listened to her talk about family.

Sitting in the third floor sauna back at the hotel I relaxed with an L & P, too tired to enjoy it. The contrast of the cement block room with a Maori Spring Sauna at Waiwera "lacked luster." I forced the experience of relaxing in water at all costs to enjoy the moment. Departure to Sydney would come quickly.

ॐ

The Days Run Together

Going forward with limitation—the best is yet to come. How similar the last three days have been in planning, closure, misinformation and some "throughs"—the energy of success running through the muck:

- ❀ John's misinformation about what was needed to inform the bank for raising the limit on ATM.

- ❀ The Ghan train planner not getting back to the airline trip planner to inform her about lack of seating. The oriental driver's wrong information about not being able to get to Waiwera.

- ❀ The bus driver thinking that 7:30 was the last ferry.

- ❀ The wrong date for the Alice Springs' hotel check-out.

At the same time, the Alice Springs Hotel made good on Monday night's snafu due to the Ghan train. The Capital One payment was not going through even though I thought it was due to an overdraft; the hotel payment pushed through for one day's withdrawal even though the withdrawal limit was over $500.00. The $80.00 US to pay for Alice Springs, plus airport tax for $25.00, plus $25.00 for the shuttle seemed to be there—just enough.

There were missed opportunities to enjoy places but people presented themselves—the university professor and the Maori bus driver. There was no side trip to the West beach but I was prepared for the trip—packed, final arrangements and pick up, vouchers, etc. and pay for a Quantas ticket to Alice Springs in the Outback.

Perhaps the best would come.

೮

The Swords
Seeing First Australians
Opposites
One with the Chinese
Art
Time to be Seen

The Swords

Coming from Scotland, Valerie admitted that Australia's energy was not her own. Even though she was far from the desert in Sydney she could feel the power of the desert air; "it is a survival land." I, too, recalled the smell of the ocean before I would get closer to the coast back home; the aura is one of elevation and inspiration. I was at the Australian beach and ocean for the afternoon—a respite from the brick and mortar of international Sydney. I would recall Hagar in the desert and the recognition of her water source being beneath her when she asked God for help. "The well is there. Drink from it." Where was my inspiration?

As Valerie read my Tarot cards, she pulled up two sword cards; on the first card swords crossed at a truce; on the second card swords pointed upward. Yesterday I saw the phrase printed on a poster, "Fire in the Belly." "My inspiration is coming related to mind and creativity," Valerie said, interpreting the words. "Does it have to do with faith and survival?" I asked. "Have faith; it is around the corner even though you are at a truce now." Find my source and my inspiration will lead me to great success? Dull with the feelings of no source for inspiration, I felt hopeless.

She removed something from my back. My energy had been withheld. I had been pulling into myself and could not understand when my trip would begin. The next day I felt a bit lighter, coming from myself but not yet connecting as much with others as I know is possible for me. There was always camaraderie but no deep joy. I was an outsider experiencing people and the sights—even the serendipity.

છ

Seeing First Australians

On the ferry the three high school girls giggled and punched each other all the way to Manley. Derrick, the younger looking teenager, did not budge when the girls dressed in low-cut tops showed their young breasts. They were on their way to a soccer game. Without judgment, they asked the boy's name and how old he was. They seemed innocent in their unconscious awareness of how lovely looking they were.

Before leaving the dock, painted aboriginals played the long wooden tubes. Forty thousand years they have been here. Although I missed staying in the Rocks section of the town, I saw it from the taxi when going to the theatre and also as the ferry pulled away. Perhaps it's okay that I am not there, staying in the midst of its sad history.

In Manley, I am at the well now like the Old Testament woman in the desert—that is the faith. However, the healer reader's cards showed a statement—"no movement. But around the corner the mind and inspiration follow with success in all areas." A second card for the mind showed "change—The Queen of Cups—emotional life high. "I needed to hear this and be raised up from a curious plateau.

છ

Opposites

Within a ten-minute walk of Chinatown, I stayed at an appropriate hotel and shopping area for me who wishes to be in the world.

I stood with Chinese young people in the pagoda at the entrance, near the lions. I was mesmerized by music of the ancient violin and flute. The musicians sold their CD's and entertained passersby with a free concert equal to a performance where the violinist had played in the Opera House. Listening transported me into my own creative spirit and I could breathe. I returned many times to hear the music, visit the bakery, and sit along the mall benches.

Tonight on return from Chinatown I stood in the hotel elevator and interviewed a couple attending the gala at the hotel across the street. The community services of Australia were meeting for dinner. Their mission, in part, was helping homeless people in Australia.

೮ා

One with the Chinese

In Chinatown the upbeat restaurant at the entrance and the tourist shops lining the main street created a busy ambience even though tourists parked themselves on benches to enjoy bakery take-out, street art, and meditating political groups.

At the red lacquer gates two lions flanked a center for Chinese community affairs. Old and young Chinese listened to the ancient violin and flute music coming from the artists playing on the steps leading to the restaurant. I stood next to them and, when there was room, sat with the Chinese on the benches inside the pagoda. I was aware that I was the only non-Chinese drawn into the music at this time. This scene and the music transported me into the spirit realm. It was the inspiration I needed for that day.

ॐ

Art

The middle-aged couple at the art museum had invited me to join them for lunch. We discussed the Margaret Pearson exhibit, WWII, isolationism, the world, and travel. We talked about the war. 2005 marks the 60th anniversary of the end of WWII.

Almost immediately we established a bond. She said, "If it had not been for the Americans, the Australians would not have known how to fight." Although her husband would not agree to giving that much credit, I felt affirmed in being an American. When I returned to the U. S. and talked about my travels, one of the residents at the nursing home testified that "those Australian boys were not afraid of anything."

The couple had traveled to Ayers Rock from Singapore. Today they were in town for the exhibit because they were staying with their daughter's dog while house-sitting. If the woman's husband did not want to travel she could travel on her own, as illustrated by her recent trip to India to learn about spices. "You'll love Alice Springs," she reassured me.

Time to be Seen

One of the places in Sydney "to see and to be seen" is on the international wharf, at the restaurant deck. Instead of walking around the wharf after my visit to the Opera House and the Royal Botanical Gardens, I sat within view of the international wharf. It was too far to walk to and I had to measure the distance in order to make it back in time to take my taxi to the airport. I still had a long way to walk and would take a taxi to my pick up at the hotel near Chinatown. Earlier in the day I had walked the entire way from Chinatown to the Royal Botanical gardens. Luckily there was a go-cart in the gardens which dumped me out at the bottom of the hill where I surprisingly faced Sydney's icon, the Opera House. I could surround it, take it in, and have my picture taken in front of it. All of this was unplanned on my extra, last day in Sydney.

At the outdoor café on the wharf nearest the Opera House, I savored my "Flat White." A jet boat cruised by and left a wake for me to loll in. The Queen Chief ferry glided out from the Circle Quay. I noted the time, 3:00 o'clock—and started toward my tourist gate in order to meet the taxi. At 4:15p.m. I would be on my way to the desert. The thought occurred that I had best check my ticket. In fact, I thought I should have done that in the morning. Perhaps I wanted to be free on my day to walk from Chinatown to the Opera House.

When I arrived at the New Zealand Air desk, I realized that I had missed my flight. This seemed serious because the connection was part of my entire international flight. The 6:15 p.m. departure time from Sydney was for a return flight from the Outback visit to fly from Sydney to Christ Church, New Zealand. Graciously the agent rescheduled my flight and made sure that I would go to the right desk for an international flight on my return. Getting to the Outback was becoming arduous. On the flip side, I had created a new day, my last one in Sydney.

ଓ

Entering desert life.

Digeradoo

Painted black-brown men sat on the ferry quay. A small crowd gathered for the sight and sound show. The swallowed sound of the digeradoo music followed me softly to the ferry boat. I was intrigued and felt I had arrived in Australia to see the aboriginals. The ferry boat horn muffled itself like the long hollow horn of the desert. I would hear ancient wailings again.

A rack of digeradoos centered on the desert backdrop of the stage. In the dark of the light and sound show I waited to be transported. The performer was not aboriginal, rather fair-skinned and blonde. As he held the long unwieldy tube, his hands gently patted its surface. He danced with it moving up and down slowly as he created sound with his breath looping down and through the back.

Sounds I had never heard before—clicking, echoes, and muted, elongated wails and gulps. Animals and weather and motion and stars and aboriginals—spirit at work in different tones and keys. The concert of simulated desert life pulled me into the Outback like the quiet of the Olgas had let me know that I was alive. There was meeting ground for life lived in nature with its creatures.

❧

Mantle of Safety—Remembering Where I Am

Entering the Uniting Church of Alice Springs fifteen minutes late, I settled onto the wooden bench near the entrance. Earlier in the week, I had spent part of an afternoon reading the memorial plaques dedicated to the earlier pioneers. I had meditated in the memorial church, dedicated to Rev. John Flynn, the Presbyterian minister who had ministered to the Outback when he developed his "mantle of safety"—the flying doctor's service. On the way through the desert to the West MacDonnell Ranges, we had stopped to honor him at the monolith stone over his and his wife's graves.

The sermon for the day was 'Journey to the Unfamiliar with Faith.' Certainly I had come to the Outback with the expectation of moving my life forward; I felt alone in Alice Springs with no sense of being led forward yet.

In front of the church in the corner hung a long brown-tone cloth banner with an appliqué picture of a chasm through which water spilled into a pool. The day before I had walked through a desert valley leading into a chasm where a pool had spilled out. The banner mentored my soul: "Let your center be filled with the love of God—water of life." The Standley Chasm was named after an early teacher who had taken on the load of teaching aboriginals in the afternoons, after her regular classes because the aboriginals had no one to teach them. She was a model for God's out-pouring love. What was my mission? Who did I love?

The banner reminded me that I was in the Australian Outback receiving from God. The preacher presented a sermon on the woman from Canaan pressing God for healing. What healing did I need? The song "Desert Stillness" gathered us together in benediction.

༄

Forty Cents

Saturday afternoon I relaxed on a bench in front of the Outback Café writing to my stepson in Chicago. I only had forty cents to buy the cowboy card at the tourist shop; the clerk accepted it. As I wrote, a large tall aboriginal man came lumbering toward me, moving fast. I scooted over so I would not have to sit next to him. It seemed like he was going "to make a landing" because he looked directly at me. I was fearful from the start when he moved toward me. The clairvoyant had told me I would experience a special learning like the woman who was taken on a trek by aboriginals and wrote her stories of "down under." I refused to entertain that kind of learning. I wondered if this were the time for me, in spite of myself?

When he sat next to me I could see his half-closed eye—permanently injured like the bird's eye I saw at the wild animal reserve in the Blue Mountains. He spoke English. I was surprised. "Could you give me forty cents—for something to eat?" I told him I did not have it, that I had spent it on a postcard. Of course, this was the truth. Almost automatically he pulled his fingers together to gesture toward his mouth. Even though he said "okay" acceptingly, I could see annoyance or frustration in his eyes.

Later, I recounted my experience to a store manager who gave freely to the aboriginals whom she knew personally. I had wondered about wanting food for forty cents? She explained that he probably wanted to make a phone call.

ॐ

Deedra

She came from a desert town, thirty to forty miles away. She described her head wound and pulled back her hair to make a part.

I saw nothing. The church lady listening to her used the right civil words and truly did wish her life well. Deedra also mentioned her jaw. Perhaps she had been abused. This conversation was acted out next to the coffee and cookie table in the fellowship hall where parishioners, visitors, and wandering aboriginal folks gathered. This scene was familiar to me from the after-service gatherings in Chicago city churches where parishioners and street people mingled to enjoy coffee.

Having listened, I walked away slowly to the side yard leading to the parking lot where Deedra joined me. As we walked, she pointed out her family members in the side yard next to the church. She and her husband were artists. "God wants you to express beauty," she confidently asserted with a British accent. "What is your name?" she asked. "Jacqueline," she called me. "Could you arrange for $5.00 to buy meat for my family?" "I am not supposed to…." I recalled from an earlier conversation about another entreaty for forty cents. "They may be able to help you inside," I pointed to the social hall. With a sense of decorum, she replied, "Later." No doubt Deedra had attended a mission school to learn her British accent and her sense of propriety.

❧

The Olgas

All we could think about was getting a cup of coffee. The bus driver lectured us "You have been waiting to see the rock!" We had looked out over the desert for four hours without much enthusiasm. About an hour before arriving at Uluru, our final destination, we pulled into the parking lot of the Olgas. From a distance we took in the massive mounds toppling over each other like huge loops of caramel-colored ribbon candy. We would stop and trek back into a chasm.

The mesa-like terrain leading up to the gradual rock incline gave me time to anticipate how it would be for me. It was a steeper climb than what I had imagined. Benches along the path made it easy for me to catch my breath as I looked up to see the erosion and caves—a mystery in hard time carved slowly.

I was slow. The group formed a snake as it slowly, steadily disappeared into the chasm. I tried to balance and conform my feet to the rough rocks and to believe I would be safe. Finally, when I was sure I did not want to risk a broken ankle or worse yet, to struggle and never get to the chasm entrance, I eased down to rest on a sandpaper rock mound.

No echo. No sound anywhere. Buffeted by soft sand all around and hard rock above I could hear silence. It was a cozy, warm, soft sound like my soul. The desert air quieted me to a place of rest and peacefulness. Shouts and laughing broke the silence when the sojourners mingled in a small group on the return trail to the bus.

The driver had prepared us, "The Olgas are thought to be more sacred than Uluru." Is the center in the rock a cleft, a hiding place for my spirit? What opened up my soul to a feeling of timelessness and peace? I did not need to enter the chasm. Its Spirit surrounded me. I would recall the prayer poem—"Desert Stillness" on Sunday in John Flynn's Memorial Church. It would be the truth I had experienced.

 co

Mountain of Aspiration

In the national park we trekked for twenty minutes on a mulch-padded path—walking fast to cover the expected forty-minute trail. I petted the fallen moss-covered trunks where I stopped for breath. The guide walked with me while the four twenty-year olds sped in front. Just the naming of the place on which I walked, "Mountain of Aspiration," solidified for me at the end of my trip that I had achieved my goal. The inner strength of freedom had pictured itself for me and I told the guide I no longer "danced up the mountain," as in my Northwest life for six years nor was I climbing a Mt. Victoria as I did at the beginning of my trip to conquer aloneness or new territory. I could hear in the name that I was free to go higher and was taking the action "to walk my talk."

After the tour, I walked down the steep hill from the motel to the neighborhood church. A large banner advertised the free Saturday night back packers' supper. The large movie screen in the front of the church beamed the words from Scripture towards us wayfarers sitting in the pews and at tables in the foyer. "I have a plan for you to give you hope and purpose." Other meaningful quotes from the world's wise followed. C.S. Lewis' idea spoke to my heart when his quote summarized the role of story: "Life has no problems to solve just stories to tell."

❧

Receiving

The foyer had begun to fill with backpackers. Eight women lined up behind long serving tables and ladled meat, pasta, and four or five kinds of fresh vegetables. There was garnish, too—cheese and parsley. There was abundance and choice—milk, tea, coffee, or cocoa. Women cared for young people. Men cleared the tables and ushered the long lines to the food tables. Several times ladies passed trays of homemade cookies among the tables and throughout the pews filled with young people who had eaten a complete dinner. People stayed to talk and laugh.

For a two-hour time young people ate well in a safe environment. They had come to Queenstown, the entertainment capital of the world, with little money. The blind piano player from the other local church in town skillfully played jazz for their enjoyment. Wisdom quotes continued to flash on a large screen to encourage them.

By seven o'clock the line into the church had dwindled and two hundred young people had filled the pews and lined the altar steps. One of the older women serving looked out over the young people; "They are happy." Christ-like, the entourage of middle and older-aged adults had given themselves without a return needed other than seeing a need met.

I joined a group of older adults and the pastor of the other church in town. I ate well, socialized, and watched "love come down." I received it, too. Like the others I was hungry for food and contact—to be known. I had saved this excursion to Queenstown until the end of my South Pacific tour but was unclear how the entertainment would come out since I did not ski. It came from watching the young and the older adults come together and being part of their world.

ℰℴ

Manifesting

In Arrowtown I boarded the bus with two ladies from the Queenstown church. We had eaten supper together at the Friday evening pasta supper. They offered me a ride back to Queenstown, twenty-five miles away. One of the women had attended her granddaughter's dance recital in Arrowtown.

While in the crystal shop in Arrowtown, the woman I sat next to on the plane coming from Christchurch on Qantas, approached me and reminded me to buy a crystal to take home. I bought a citrine for prosperity.

Earlier in my trip Dorothy and the lecturer at Canterbury both "showed up;" they had similar professional backgrounds to my former life in academia. Dorothy, I met on the ferry to Davenport and Ailene, I met in Sydney at an Italian restaurant where she dined alone because her friend did not show; I joined her.

ℰℴ

Next to the Last Day

Because my checking account showed a low balance, I decided to divide my apricots for the next day and eat one half of them in the evening. I began my meal with a double hot chocolate. With whole wheat bread, I fixed two pieces of toast with margarine and raspberry jelly and marmalade. The toast was like a dinner. Dessert followed with hot tea and apricots. Later I learned that I had enough to go out for dinner because a friend had deposited money in the account.

I had wanted to take the steamer to a sheep ranch on the other side of the lake. A special dinner would have been in order to celebrate the end of my time in Queenstown. When I had checked, the advertised dinner special was cancelled because of low tourist trade. The next morning it had been re-scheduled; after all, it would have been available and I would have had the money. Had I not been limited in my thinking and had I been willing to take the risk, I would have inquired more and learned of the new opening hour. This was a good lesson in the way to think and act.

I could not sleep so I got up and fixed an iced tea from the earlier pot of tea. Since leaving Auckland and Sydney, I had felt alone. There were many people to connect with and be with from all over the world. We encountered for a short while and went on. A New Zealand bookstore clerk in Christchurch observed that maybe New Zealanders were so friendly because they are lonely; they are glad to see outsiders.

ॐ

My Last Free Day in the South Pacific

After eating my muesli left over from yesterday, I abandoned the remaining apricots and scurried to get my bag packed and stored it in the office for a 10:00 a.m. checkout. Hoping I would find a non-tourist atmosphere, I passed up several bargains to take in my film to be developed and get down to the wharf. I longed for a "Flat White" on the dock in the sun, but waiting for it would make me late.

Others sitting at the tables were enjoying beverages so I stepped into the nearest shop to find only juices and yogurts and fruit smoothies. I chose a boysenberry-banana and drank it on board. Having given up on breakfast and lunch I took up the idea from a New Zealand couple and ordered pumpkin soup with a hot roll. Pitchers of ice water with lemon were available, like in the spa area in Henma. After the steamer ride, the couple I had met disappeared into their walk behind the Colonel's House restaurant on the sheep farm. I longed to get off and enjoy the area.

After the lake ride, on my return to Queenstown shore I strolled along the pebbly public beach and found a lovely restaurant with a deck overlooking the lake beneath the mountain. How I enjoyed the lull of the water and the dogs fetching a stick. Speedboats lolled in the currents waiting for later crews. Air and space and nature surrounded me. The hotels and shops stacked on the hillside. My dinner was served—a lovely salmon pie on top of potatoes and green vegetables with a cheese top and crème dressing.

Time was short and I packed in every good thing. Instead of dessert I finally enjoyed a "Flat White" and a candy bar, so that I could hurry across the street to a modern design shop. Ironically, it turned out to be the oldest building in Queenstown, a unique substitute for the Colonel's sheep farmhouse I missed.

8

I visited three sheep areas on the South Island. Peacefulness pictured for me.

Flying

- ✈ 903 km/hr ground speed
- ✈ 4:54 time to destination
- ✈ 5:01 local time
- ✈ Just crossed the dateline at Apia!!
- ✈ 10,1000m. Altitude
- ✈ -40 degree c. temperature outside
- ✈ 2,954 km from departure
- ✈ Auckland Sydney and Melbourne about the same latitude.
- ✈ I am headed to the equator

℘

Blue Hawaii

A breakthrough today—the ocean appeared blue, light navy and turquoise. I enjoyed a smoothie on the lanai at the Sheraton near where I had lunch before my trip started—a chicken quesadilla—not as scrumptious as the first time—but the ocean view was what I ordered. Only a few children below were falling and rolling in the waves.

Girls from Adelaide vacationed on the lanai. I had been diverted from Adelaide when the Ghan connection to Alice Springs fell through at the last minute. Now I could connect with folks from Adelaide. We talked about story, Patty's love of writing and JoAnna's grandmother.

Finally, my place of rest became the tree trunk on the beach. I crawled underneath the low branches and propped against the gnarled trunk to continue reading my new novel, *The Mermaid Chair*. It was serendipitous for me to find and choose my chair and novel on my last afternoon at the beach before my evening flight. I had wanted to create a unique experience before take-off.

ɞ

No Limitation

Steel-blue water. Diamond Head poses majestically in the sun. Ridges from top to bottom—gentle folds peaking. By contrast, the white angular hotel at the tip of the island cuts into the range. Train-like clouds puff their small gray tufts of used-up smoke over Waikiki. I believe I will see the sunset and feel relaxed.

ɞ

Mantle of Safety

Literal travel represents my dreams and heart's desires and the transcendency of my mind and soul. The events of travel enable me to live out the person I truly am. The events help me express and see the internal self. During flight, the serendipitous shows me that I am on the right track. My heart's desires get refined and defined by circumstances. I work out what needs to grow or be changed by adapting to situations.

CHAPTER VII

Testaments

"Reluctant to say good-bye to the bird I saw that he fell behind as I drove forward. To my surprise another bird was ahead and I saw that I would catch up with him. Beyond flew another messenger leading the way. The Heron was my Holy Spirit who I pictured was guiding me, always abiding... ."

Breakfast on the trail in the Colorado Rockies—our best family vacation.

CHAPTER VII

Testaments

Inspire

My life inspires me. The stories I preserve assure me of its continuity, direction, and success. Even as a high school teacher I was able to be a practitioner and a theoretician. I knew that the context for my practical work was my own theory. Naturally, in my doctoral research I developed a theoretical worldview which grew from life practice and used illustrations from interdisciplinary resources spanning the gamut of religious philosophy to common life art. Loving our farm and the writings of Willa Cather about the land inspired me to write about the phenomenon of "loving the land." Showing how the relationship transpired motivated me.

"Mother's Field." When she was in a wheelchair, we followed the baler while riding in the car; she could reach and feel the bales after they were dropped. Friends of the farm kept track of the number of cuttings each season and would tell me.

Growing up in a Midwestern rural community I acquired work ethics and a "grounded" orientation which has made it possible for me, in general, to play tether ball with the sky—to adopt wings, imagination and spirit. Thus *Flight Beyond the Stars* has become airborne because of these following testaments to my everyday life. I invite the reader to examine the everyday so as to travel life's distances and to see the "stars at noon," as Cochran did, but also "to fly beyond the stars."

Life experiences while putting up peaches, taking the cat to the vet, caring for my mother and walking the boundaries of the farm with my father are as important to me as walking the Magnificent

Mile in Chicago and meeting a vagrant who had one hand, climbing Mt. Rainier from the Paradise entrance, or flying toward the equator on my way home from New Zealand. Both the small and apparently far away lead me home to my everyday life and its far reaches into spiritual discernment and fulfillment.

I believe I am entitled to years of a mystical life because of my familiarity and enmeshment with the everyday vicissitudes and requirements of life, both pleasant and difficult. I tend to deal with the difficult in life—divorce, unemployment, death, litigation, and separation—sometimes simultaneously—so that I seem always to have a full plate. I take it on, like it, and succeed through it. I am a bit like my lawyer father who thrived on a good fight; he was a former boxer. I live through these situations and write about healing them with animals. The nature parables in *Beneath the Tall Black Door* illustrate predicaments in life's maneuvering which are assisted by the messages which wild animals bring when they appear at just the time a solution is needed—overworking, losing loved ones, chemical dependency, losing faith, finding life's mission.

When life is viewed as a whole, a transcendent perspective of the Eagle is possible and we are aware of the transcendency of down-to-earth temporal experience joining the eternal quality of our lives. Of course, our lives exist simultaneously in both dimensions whether we see it or not.

"Flying high" is an escape at times but more so I think it is a balancing of my heart's desires because I excel in the inclusion of all of life's demands and pleasures. My plate is generally and genuinely full three-fourths of the time. I seem to be free enough to fly to Honolulu for twenty-four hours or hike through the woods on Mt. Aspiration in New Zealand because of the demands and pleasures. Perhaps I will evolve to all pleasure and hedonism and abandon my Midwest work ethic but it is doubtful because both seem essential for understanding unity in existence.

It is easy to believe that the same old rut in life continues or that familiar places do not offer the mystical. For example, when I would return to the Northwest after being on the Big Island, I perceived my community paling compared to white sandy beaches with tropical air-filled fragrances. The gray lakes of the Northwest Sound could not compare with the variegated blue bands of the Pacific Ocean.

Where do I turn for inspiration in my Midwestern hometown after the mountains and streams of Vermont, my second home? This weekend my partner returned to the Northeast and I was left with the responsibility of caring for mother and all household responsibilities. I drove north from the bus station toward my former home in the university town where I received my PhD There was nothing to take away now—"been there; done that." Instead, I let myself get lost, as I used to do twenty years ago, in the rich flat fields. I would see forever into the horizon. My mind could clear and I could find peace in earth.

Stopping at a filling station to buy Schwend's mint ice cream, I explained to the other customers the mind-clearing that I had done. Driving on, I found the Comfort Inn in Amish territory. Next door, I ate Mexican beans for supper and returned to a cozy room where I rested from my life. The next day I had to be up by 8:00 a.m. to help my mother at the hospital. The morning of her dismissal I needed to be available to see the doctor. First, I would need to drive for two hours and eat breakfast. My heart would be as clear as my mind at 5:30 a.m.

Inspiration has also come from learning through people. I have always learned from the most humble teachers; the man with the scarred hand who displayed his gold cross; the one-handed piano player who begged for money near "the Magnificent Mile;" the drunken woman who reached out with one hand to connect with me and exclaimed, "Happy Mother's Day." May I be so humble to meet others and may I take my humility to move to a place of greatness. The hometown bakery waitress on Sunday passed on to me her mother's wisdom: "Don't forget to be great—that's what God wants for you."

"Christening of my brother and me." I was embarrassed because
I was an older child. Both sets of grandparents and great-
grandparents on my father's side (center) attended the event at
the Methodist Church in our village north of Chicago.

Easter Morning's new frocks.

Spring Arrives

I went on a getaway weekend. As it ended I was driving down the River Road and saw a Blue Heron paralleling the car next to the driver's side. Earlier in the morning I had read an inspirational book on letting God guide by showing instead of looking for answers to all the complex problems. *Reluctant to say good-bye to the bird I saw that he fell behind as I drove forward. To my surprise another bird was ahead and I saw that I would catch up with him. Beyond flew another messenger leading the way. The heron was my Holy Spirit who I pictured was guiding me, always abiding,* because the heron was on the bird-box each morning at my home on the lake in the Northwest.

ဢ

The Only Girl

I grew up a tomboy because there were no other girls in the neighborhood, except for fifth graders; my dad wanted a boy. Being tough meant not crying no matter how much I got hurt. Although I do not remember any incidents specifically, I have blocked them out; I do remember an adult incident when my brother visited my house in Urbana. We both lived there during graduate school.

The garage door wedged my fingers when it folded in half. I showed no emotion. My brother said that it had to hurt. Actually, I think I was in shock and could not feel it. Maybe the same thing happened in the neighborhood.

ဢ

The northern neighborhood gang near my grandmother's house, three blocks from our home; best friends on the left, arm in arm.

Collecting Locust Shells

Lattice walls enclosed a dirt floor play area underneath the porch of my neighbor friend's house. On the ledges of the 2 x 4's we grew collections of locust skeletons. Wiling away summer afternoons after school we added to our cicada collections. We competed about the number of cicada skeleton shells we had lined up.

We girls talked about sex a lot in fifth grade even though I was in first grade. My observations were about dogs, as I recall. My friends and I were afraid that the mean boys would invade us if they found our secret hideout under the porch. I do not think sex was an issue but hurting us physically was the fear. They had reputations for being mean boys.

The Tumbling Award

When I was in grade school, on Saturday morning at the old college gym approximately thirty children swarmed to do somersaults, flips, and backbends. Our college-age teacher involved us as teachers of *younger* children and as performers in a dance recital to be held at the junior high gymnasium.

Snow White in our dance recital.

For the teaching assistants our mentor rewarded improvement by a personal visit to her dorm room. She gave the biggest reward to three of us in the eighth grade. During the summer we went home with her to Northern Illinois for a vacation on Lake Michigan.

I met my first beau, a tall, handsome lifeguard who was a dreamboat. The relationship continued when he came to my hometown to be part of the dance recital where we performed together.

This winter I reread his letters. "Maybe later," he wrote. I had asked him to marry me! Marriage was on my mind at a young age.

Canceling the Field Trip

In high school I was a leader. The Social Studies class had planned a field trip for the entire class to visit Greenville civic centers. It had involved a tremendous amount of work for me to arrange and contact businesses and to prepare the class. On the day before or the day of the trip, the class was misbehaving and the teacher canceled the outing. For me, it was undermining and a big letdown. I remember fleeing down the hall in tears; another teacher encouraged me to see the principal. The event was reinstated but I lost some trust in adult decisions because I was in an adult role without any say-so. However, I do not think there was any retribution and we succeeded in the project.

℘

I learned to lead in high school. Recently I felt that I had no influence on others. Serendipitously, at the hospital gift shop, a volunteer recounted how her daughter had admired me leading cheers and spent all afternoon making a pom-pom like mine. She wanted to be like me; her name was Jackie, too. Today she is a teacher.

Holding the Door

The high school boys were big and husky compared to petite me, their teacher. Someone asked me how someone as small as I could get them to do what I wanted. Of course, I did not always. During the seventies we integrated for the first time. My classroom was in the basement with few other classrooms nearby. Feelings ran high—there was a fight outside my door in the hall. Inside, the white guys were determined to protect their friends. It was my responsibility to keep order by preventing them from going out the door. I plastered myself against it. They stopped. It took me a long time to get over the feelings of helplessness.

ॐ

Angel in Disguise

Every teacher has students who are difficult to relate to and to teach—sometimes in the same person. Heavy student loads and nine-week class changes demanded intense "speeded up knowing" of my students, personally and academically. A problem-behavior girl sat to the left near my desk. Ordinarily unfriendly, on one day she was particularly withdrawn. I would have welcomed the quiet except that she was extremely "down." Immediately after class I ran up to the counselor's office in the short five minutes I had to get there and back to my room. Later in the day when I followed up with the counselor, she related as much as she could. The girl's life had probably been saved by the intervention. I had moved on to more students and more problems later in the day but remembered how significant it was "to be the responsible party."

&

Terminal Teacher

They assigned me to teach the students not bound for college. In those days, the class was called "terminal" because most of the students did not continue in school beyond high school. Because I was an alternative teacher I could individualize and create groups and independent study for students who had not been recognized for their abilities or creativity. The students gladly met the challenge presented to them of using college-bound materials at a different pace. After seven years I burned out.

The most heart-warming experience was to watch a circle of African American boys telling a story. Because they became involved in listening to a good story, they could remember and retell it verbatim in a circle around our improvised campfire.

&

Rapunzel, Come Down

After twelve years of teaching high school, I asked for a two-year leave of absence to complete my doctorate. Because I was valued in the district, they gave me an unprecedented two years. However, when I returned, I felt devalued when I was "kicked upstairs" to the tower—the highest room in the high school, totally isolated with no windows and a long climb up three flights of stairs. The ironic demotion from basement to tower was my cue for flight. A few days before school, I resigned and joined my husband in an out-of-town job. My old job seemed impossible. Rapunzel came down and fled with Prince Charming.

"Going places" on a teachers' weekend get-away.

Talking over teaching plans with a prospective teacher;
a payoff for my career in teacher education.

Artist Residency

My teacher friend was an encourager. "You should send your stories to *Good Housekeeping*." For three sessions, which was most of the day, we led her students in listening to my stories, writing their own, and illustrating both. She reviewed writing skills for end-of-the-year study.

I had been her "sub" teacher many times and so I made plans to see her at the beginning of the week after coming home from Vermont. In the living room on Friday, Dad showed me the *Advocate* article on a Sorento teacher who had died in an accidental shooting during a war re-enactment with her family.

Quietly, I read Judy's story realizing how my teacher friend—creative, innovative—was a victim of a senseless error. The incident portrayed her innocence.

ಬ

Remembering Judy
For her generosity and caring spirit,
Her creativity in teaching
and love and support of students
and fellow teachers

Jams and Jellies

Buying produce from Amish farms became a hobby when I had an upright freezer. Twenty years later, I returned to the area on a county road to retrace my route to the farm where I bought pecans. I could see there was a jelly stand hut near the house. I remembered the lady who had invited me in for her goat cheese.

In the shed lot, a man told me that his wife was inside. She received me and introduced me to her thirteen-year-old daughter who was learning how to sew at a table off the living room. When I told her I had been a customer twenty years ago, she was thrilled to recount the years since her latest child and "to meet someone who remembered her when she was young."

ॐ

We "children" in my mother's kitchen on the farm.

Mother visiting the kitchen in my first house

Making Custard

Doing for my Dad never stopped. Mother had had a stroke and it was helpful, but stressful, to have me home. Our personality and age differences seemed to get in the way.

Nonetheless, I made custard for the first time because my dad loved it. His mother had made it and my mother did not. At least, I do not remember it. It was so easy that I could not believe that I could be so domestic in my fifties. This was a breakthrough in my culinary confidence, not unlike feeling I could make an angel food cake with my mother, albeit from a box. A first for both of us, we were proud of ourselves. Our cake.

ଓ

Oyster Stew

When the New Year came in, Dad, Hans, and I celebrated New Year's Eve of 2000 together. Mother had always prepared oyster stew on Christmas Eve and also New Year's Eve because Dad loved it so much. Because Mother was staying in the hospital's extended care unit, the tradition was now mine to carry on.

Instead of homemade broth, I bought Campbell's oyster stew and added butter, canned oysters and half-and-half. Dad thought it was delicious and he continued making his stew with my new method. The best part was that we all felt the tradition remained— not all had been lost when life brought changes and loss.

ଓ

Food Over Time

I planted spring and fall gardens in my L-shaped plot next to the house. One year when I did not care so much about depending on the vegetables, I marketed at the shopping center plaza because I had planted potatoes which took up half of the garden. When they were ready to harvest, like "going for gold" or buried treasure, I dug large circles around each plant after I found one or two or three potatoes. Truly the potatoes were "apples of the earth" with their stems and their round bodies. I felt like a farmer; probably I identified with earth-bound characters from Pearl Buck's novels.

ॐ

Grandma Kelsey said the family would call me its "pet."

Don't Stand Out

There was a six-year difference between my sister and me. I was the cute baby and the family considered me its "pet," according to my little Grandma.

Although my sister was talented, I was led to minimize my own talents so as not to hurt her feelings.

Therefore, I grew up feeling thwarted. My self-confidence was at a low level anyway. My father did not want to have favorites so everything was equal. It seemed unfair not to have acknowledged sufficiently my accomplishments so that I could feel honored.

A Wife Follows Her Husband

The night before I announced to my first husband that I was ending the marriage—leaving him and our new house—it was clear that my conscience would not permit me to continue being together. I thought it was difficult for him to keep up with my dominant personality and aspirations, even though he was in a PhD program and I was only teaching. I thought I would hold him back.

I doubt that his mother had divorce in mind when she declared out of the blue at lunch, "a wife should follow her husband." She undoubtedly wanted the best for us. I was frantically trying to finish my MA degree while teaching and supporting us in a second and third year of marriage. The first year, my father-in-law supported us because he did not want me to have to work like his wife had to when she put him through medical school.

&

The Walnut Business

In junior high, my friend and I wanted to make money and decided to hull walnuts from the farm woods and sell them in plastic bags.

We collected and pounded the green tennis balls, threw them at cement walls. Finally we would free a nut. It seemed endless to crack the nuts and pick out the pieces. We persevered.

Our hands were black for days. We charged fifty cents a bag. With our six bags, three each, we were dirt-poor and "nutty."

&

You are a Survivor

When I was in graduate school working on my doctorate, I lived on a shoestring budget. I cannot imagine having so little money that I would not have a reserve of $15 but I must have enjoyed making ends meet and making it with ingenuity.

On a weekend I took the train to Chicago to visit my sister. I had the fare from Effingham to Chicago but had not thought about and did not have enough for the commuter train from the downtown station to the northern suburb.

I decided to trade my postage stamps for cash and so I ventured into a nearby Eddie Bauer store to try bartering. Without hesitating, a young college-age clerk swapped his cash for my stamps.

ॐ

The farm road near the persimmon tree where Dad told the story about saving the farm.

Walking the Boundaries

Last summer Dad, Hans and I walked down to the pond and back up to the hill, above the road that winds by the Post House. We sat near the persimmon tree where the 1820's pioneer family built their home.

Dad again told the story about the division of the farm. Mother would not take her part in cash but in land only. When she did that, Grandma decided to take hers in land. Dad had stopped the sale by the farm agent. The agent said, "You cannot do this." Dad replied, "I can and I will."

My mother and her youngest sister drew straws for their pieces of land. Each received a hill, field, and woods.

The grandson of a farm tenant heard loud barking in the woods while he was driving on the farm road late at night after work. He hiked back to the silo only to find a small hound dog that could not get out of the silo.

Our two-car garage was made from the old barn wood. Dad had a sign made for the front – 1858. When I was the age pictured, I went to the barn by myself and fled when I heard a bum in the barn.

The old hog barn became a horse stable with a paddock which opened out into the woods.

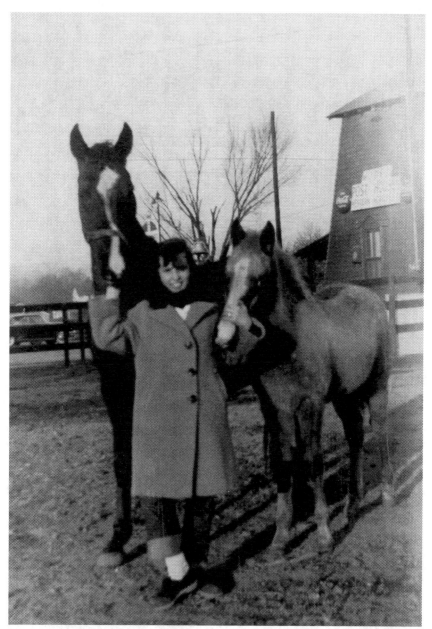

"Queen Titania and her foal, Gladworthy King." I helped feed them when we kept them in the paddock around the Post House when it was in town. On the farm, they stayed in the hog barn and paddock.

The interior of the hog barn suggested open living; an area the length of the barn with partial room divider-like stalls along the side. The drawing I made of a future house suggested by the hog barn became a reality in the Apple Shed fifty years later.

The woods became our family playground – mushroom hunting, fishing, picking wildflowers, and picnics. We hosted my college senior picnic in the woods. Dad harvested walnut trees and sold them in Switzerland.

Dad driving his Lo-Boy with a new load for the woodpile.

I took walks near the barn with Dad frequently to see if the well pump was running. Water availability was always a concern. When my parents built their home on the hill, two lakes would not hold water so they "witched" a well near the house. The well never went dry.

A Cemetery Visit Tradition Gone

On Thanksgiving the family would target-shoot on the fence line toward the woods and usually a group walked over to the Blanchard pioneer cemetery.

The Blanchards are like kin. The farm has been in three families, theirs, my grandfather's, and his heirs for 185 years. Our families are one in time with a spirit of development.

This fall there is a new owner of half the hill including the old farm building sites, the remnants on the landscape, and the cemetery. The silo and cement watering tank of the 1860's are part of my childhood landscape and experiences on the farm. The new owners posted "No Trespassing" signs near the clear cutting where the field ridge cemetery is; the ridge is gone now, too. My grandfather Andrews had created it.

The stones stand without covering because the trees were removed to develop the surrounding farm ground. The new fence around them allows snow to pack up. My memory has become sharper and serves me to keep an essential connection and tradition. The genealogy society had the stones repaired several years ago. I worry about the safety and longevity of the stones. Grief.

ॐ

Blanchard Family Cemetery, drawing by the late Robert Horsfall, local artist.

Drawing Commissioned by author, presented at the Apple Shed in 2009, on the occasion of fifty years since the author's high school graduation.

Seth Blanchard house built circa 1822.

I remember it from childhood when I swung on a board hanging from the side yard tree. A fire bush from the Blanchard side yard grows near the tracks at the Apple Shed.

All of the Blanchard children were married at their family home on top of the hill. My wedding reception in June 1963 was held in the yard on top of the adjacent farm hill (once apple orchard), over one hundred years later.

Daughter, Almira Blanchard, educated in Vermont, co-founded Almira College, which was predecessor to the town's Liberal Arts College. I graduated from the same College, following in the tradition of the Andrews' girls and their husbands and some children, great uncle and both grandparents. Just as my father was caretaker of the farm, he also shepherded the college as a long-time trustee and legal counselor.

"New married life."

Putting Up Peaches

We were poor when I was in graduate school and lived off of my husband's income. Anxious to get a bargain I bought bushels of fruit from the Amish when the fruit was beyond table-ready but good for putting up. Of course, I bought too much. About 11:00 in the evening I would give out on the peeling and cutting and sugaring for the freezer syrup.

Not wanting the fruit to go to waste, my husband would stay up until 2:00 in the morning to finish the peaches. He would beg me not to get so much next time. Of course, I knew if I did, he would finish the job and therefore, I kept on buying.

෫ర

A Triathlon of Jobs

At Christmas time, my husband left without calling for three weeks because of a disagreement about when to have his children to celebrate Christmas. Because we had not been getting along for sometime, this was a convenience for him to withdraw. I made up my mind to be self-sufficient and independent financially even though I was not finished with my PhD dissertation.

A full- time job for the semester came along at a university fifty miles away. A dictum to finish the PhD research shortly followed so I had only February and March to pull it together in final form for submission to the graduate college the first week in April.

Although all went well I was getting up at 4:00 a.m. to edit, drive fifty miles, and teach all day. I also returned mid-week to teach an evening graduate level class. We had built toward graduation for eight years.

"A family graduation."

We three family women were professionals.

After graduation, I taught summer school to Japanese students in a language-cultural experience program. They excelled. Before it ended, I had to move to Missouri to start a new fall job for the year.

ℰ

Epiphany

Last year at Christmas we were at odds. The pressure was on with decorating, social activities at school, flying back to the Midwest. We did not have time to set aside for our gift giving and we did not want to give to each other because of the arguing. We decided to wait until after Christmas to exchange gifts.

It took until Epiphany for us to get in the appropriate mood to give each other a gift. We had gone to Quebec City to rest and be festive after our sojourn to the Midwest with family. We stepped into an Episcopal English-speaking church on Epiphany Sunday and listened to the minister remind us that we bring our personal gifts to Christ. Reading more in the encyclopedia when we returned home, we were turned on to writing a Christmas letter and celebrating our new-found awareness of Christ being honored by Kings as THE KING. We opened our gifts to each other.

❧

Being Received

When I decided to buy the old gray garage from my family, people in my hometown said such personal things to me that I felt like a hometown girl again. One woman suggested I could use it for myself as a place to have coffee. Another asked me if I were "playing house." A local realtor said he knew I would do something creative. Others have commented on how creative it looked with the mural painting on the east end. Besides seeing me taking care of my mother at the nursing home, this was my first community contribution—a way for people to see who I am. The college-age painting of me displayed in the window at the Apple Shed prompted one of the nurses at the nursing home to ask how old I was in the painting—"young."

ℬ

Make Your Inch

Whenever I would get discouraged (because I would take on too much) Mother would remind me of Grandpa Andrews' saying, "Make your inch each day."

The beautiful, musically talented Andrews sisters, all professional women, with their Mother who taught Latin and designed beautiful clothes for them. My grandparents offered them all the opportunities they did not have growing up. Grandpa was a handsome, sensitive man. He wrote a poem about each of his daughters—their personalities, gifts, and potential. He said my mother would have friends all of her life, and she did.

My cousin reprinted Grandpa's diary when her mother passed on. Grandpa's "inch" was clear in the portrayal of his journey from teenager, walking to farm work fifty miles away, to college teaching, followed by staking a claim in South Dakota with Grandma, who lived by herself for a year in the claim shack; to building a hardware business, building the glove factory, and buying farms—along with his marriage and rearing of his five beautiful daughters, all musically talented and well educated. (Imogene, his sixth daughter died during infancy.) It is a coincidence that he came from a family of six boys and three girls.

Our cousins' reunion visit to Grandma's house on the avenue; we cousins are "get" from my mother and her older sister.

My young parents enjoyed leisure, picnics, outings,
and home suppers with friends.

Mother and Dad bought my Grandfather's glove factory. They ran the factory and when they closed the business Dad used the offices for his law practice. Mother had run the sewing room but continued to help him in the office, until she started teaching English full time. After retiring she managed the offices of Dad's law practice in the Kelsey Building. They stand next to a plaque honoring their parents. I helped my father write portions of his life story in the office. "John Is It All Right?" was characteristic of a client's need for reassurance and fitting for his life work, to make it right.

Cousins visiting Dad's office and their grandfather's former office in the Model Glove Company.

When we were young, staying at our cousins' home in St. Louis, was a highlight. My aunt always entertained us with a play, visit to the flower show, or a special restaurant like The Green Parrot.

(Make Your Inch, continued)

Recently, I bought the service building for the glove factory and "inch my way" to refurbishing it for a story center, a place for me to hang my hat on.

My own life has inched from teaching and supervising student teachers to getting a PhD, to jumping hoops in the university system, to becoming a writer/storyteller and a guide to others to tell their stories; and finally to becoming a world traveler and "miracle worker" in everyday life.

℘

The Eagle's Watch

I selected the stories in Chapter VII from three volumes of my life stories. They tell the story of my sense of humility and greatness. I am like you but I fly ahead to show you what you can see and know more of in your life. You have traveled distance, literal or not, and deserve to know that all of it holds together, takes you somewhere you want to go and be, and that you are aware of the parts and the whole. I propose that you can go farther—you can transcend and connect your life to the eternal nature of it and thus certainly you can fly beyond the stars, through the dark, to your wholeness and creativity, connecting with the world through travel and study. Realizing the miracles of everyday life and writing about them can be one of your greatest achievements.

EPILOGUE

Surrender to Light

When there is no fit, is it a surprise since there exists, uniquely, only you? What more can you do but to stand at the edge of creation and sing, like Milton's picture of the dove, hovering over the abyss? You, too, create. Bowing to the light and beauty of God, you are engulfed with the wholeness. JKK

"Surrender to Silver Light"

Surrender to Light
Celebrating the Flight to Creativity
on "The Magnificent Mile" of Eternity
Prayer in Celebration of Wholeness

EPILOGUE

Surrender to Light

What I have in common with Cinderella is the desire to be accepted, because I always felt like the black sheep of my family, unconventional and a bit unruly, independent, argumentative, when needed.

I have experienced the sibling rivalry syndrome. Where did Cinderella get her strong self-concept to bring her prince to her? In counseling I used to say I would rise above situations, whereupon, I was encouraged to hit the matter head-on. Throughout life I have been hitting matters head-on.

Contrastingly, I have levitated with success in my own carriage in the fairytale land of healing, the Big Island, Hawaii. One time I sensed that I had left my body while driving around the north end along the coast at sunset. The car and I moved on separate energies but together in the same space and at the same speed. I am a metaphysician seeing and explaining beyond the visible, seeing beyond the stars. Transcending thought to a circular understanding of the universe and man's capacity for faith, I completed theory research and the development of a philosophical worldview on imagination.

Winging life as I did in the story "Sometimes You Have to See the Ocean" I unconsciously created a Cinderella experience of rising above the demands of reality, asking them to move over to enable serendipity to reign so that I could soar. The magic of the show, literally, and the experience with dance, including the hula, has been required for me to become who I really am through dancing up the mountain, flying from the summit and reaching beyond the stars into the dark.

Flyer Jacqueline Cochran has been called "Cinderella of the Air." My namesake, always a princess, received world recognition for accomplishments in expressing the person she truly was, a beautiful adventurer and humanitarian—a phoenix rising from the ashes of poverty. Like her, I am a bird in flight with the vision of my totem animal, Red Hawk. Last week he reminded me of this truth by flushing himself from the roadside and flying within a foot of my windshield. I could not miss the flight to bring me out of life's hard circumstances.

I transcend earth and sky; and like Cochran in her book who describes seeing "stars at noon," I travel at a depth and height and depth to be one with all, especially the "creepy crawlies" that I run with. There are omissions in story topics and themes which have created the bedrock strength which guided me to a mountain ascent—my ancestors' dedication to God and their example of providing for the learning needs of others. For example, my grandmother's brother who became an officer in a Chicago steel company, founded a vocational school outside of the city for boys from the city who might be overlooked. He got funding to provide the best in laboratory equipment and teachers. Moreover, he sought the best for me when he influenced me as a young teenager to seek excellence in choosing Oberlin College for undergraduate studies and Leland Stanford for graduate work.

The most hidden and influential part of my life is our belief that the family has Native American roots, in part. Many signs point toward the truth. Our life-long family friends in the Midwest had close connections to Native Americans because the woman's father was an administrator on several reservations and she grew up on a reservation. We brought "Black Forest," our five-gaited gelding and "Pot o' Gold," a Tennessee Walker, back to our farm from a reservation in Oklahoma where our friend's father had been an administrator. We connected by friendship and interests.

Dad and I on "Pot o' Gold," champion, Tennessee Walker.

Also, I recognized the spirit of dance howling in me when the Indian mascot for the Illini danced the length of the football field at my alma mater university. In childhood and adulthood I saw Indian dancing at the Wisconsin Dells, simulating real Native American dancers as they disembarked canoes off the river to perform the Corn Dance.

No wonder that I sought tribal powwows, the dance of life, to inspire me in the Northwest when I lived through a six-year transition which I know to have been like the shaman's which Joseph Campbell describes in *The Power of Myth*.

Community story told through the husband of our family friends verified for me the truth of my native heritage. When he asked his mother, who would have known old-timers and stories about everyone for years back, he reported that she said, "There is no doubt about their Native American Heritage." This would have been mid-1800's life story.

Therefore, I can understand my love of the land reaching deeper than our family's farm and pioneer heritage. My Native connection to the soil drove me to the deep connection I understand and illustrate through doctoral research on imagination, spirituality and the land.

Several years after I was in the Northwest, I returned for a visit and I was privileged to read a paper written by a Sioux man whose tenets and support were identical in understanding. Naturally, I understand mysteries of native peoples in Hawaii, New Zealand, and Australia. Naturally I understand parallel universes, the oneness of time and space, and a circular worldview of life. My mind and heart find residence beyond the stars because I am one with God's tangible substance, the earth.

"Surrender to Silver Light"

The lines of traffic slowed to a stop at the entryway under the stone Peace Arch, grand like the Arc de Triomphe in Paris. People draped out of their cars to cool off. Others had escaped to the entryway gardens; reluctantly they ambled back to their cars. My Jeep was parked on an inner lane next to a car of Japanese girls.

I was on a mission to find a new direction for my life. All of my creative efforts and successful workshops were not leading me to make a living. I would visit the university to find the department building where my former doctoral professor now taught. Because she had made praising comments about my scholarship and, because I admired her, I sought out the place as a place of encouragement, for take off; perhaps in spirit only. I was acknowledging and returning to my intellectual prowess, training and former career, as a resource for my professional success.

The Japanese girls and I fanned each other, laughing and sharing breathy, hot sighs. When the traffic ahead began to roll, we jerked forward, side by side. All of a sudden the air stirred above us and we ducked under. From the left over the huge peace arch soared a mature bald eagle with its enormous wing spread. It whirred the air as if it were a low flying plane. We signaled to each other—I had to lean towards the rider's seat window to share the wonder with the girls—we saw it together. Back to the driver's seat to see it again and back to the window on the other side. The eagle soared in its path directly over our cars. Wow! What an entry we made through the Peace Arch "under an eagle's wings," when I needed to soar. Many times in the past when I needed a new beginning I had signaled to the bird of the East, an omen of creativity, from my loft apartment on the water; the juvenile and mature eagles would fly by my picture windows almost at the moment of my request for help. They nested in the nearby woods off the lakeshore.

On the campus I asked the students about the location of Lauren's class building. After climbing three flights of stairs, I stood in front of her office complex. Of course, I knew she would not be there; it was after five o'clock, but I was preparing myself for a later visit. Merely seeing the place gave me courage to see myself as she had seen me several years ago. Hallway posters advertised the graduation celebration at a downtown hotel; probably Lauren would be there. I was not dressed to go nor did I want her to actually see me. I would write to her when I got home.

Evening was closing in. I had a three-hour drive home. Even so I would choose the beautiful mountain drive alongside the water after I crossed over the border. The sun was setting and the islands in the South appeared like giant humped sea mammals in the misty gray sky. The sky-colored water rippled silver streaks. Through forested embankments, partial shafts of light cut through to me as I slowed the car and tried to see more water and light at each clearing. Several times I pulled over to open the shutter wider. As the clouds let the sun create more gold and silver water, I became mesmerized. I could not see or get enough.

The car found the next clearing by itself. I jumped out and sat on a rock to brace myself for a panoramic view. The greatness of the beauty took over my soul and I heaved from a hallowed cave, whose bellows deep inside whooshed out non-sound. Was it the hollow of the empty stovepipe in me, which could not hold sound? No. It was like the children's story when the animal ate up sound, swallowing its own guttural. How unlike the glee I heard from my dog, Gigi, when she groaned with her whole body welcoming me home the last time I saw her.

The sound I felt was anguish when I realized my finiteness in the majesty and infiniteness of God. Surrendering myself in the face of His beauty, I rocked myself to calmness from crying that seemed it would never find a hearer, a witness. Perhaps I also had heard the beauty and it had consumed me with a greater knowing. I died in the beauty of God.

The Eagle of the East had signaled a new beginning and light. Passing through the Peace Arch a second time had led me to a water-born fracturing of spirit light to which I could surrender my spirit and be led to a new focus.

Celebrating seventy years of life I view life like I saw the silver light on the mountain drive—partially and gradually. At age seventy I have seen at least two thirds of life from earth. I still maintain a perspective which gives me continuity in flight through time and also, beyond the stars' timelessness, through the dark.

ॐ

Celebrating the Flight to Creativity on the "Magnificent Mile" of Eternity

- Aboard the Texas Eagle, I chose the view car for a five-hour ride to Chicago.

- Checking into the hotel suite, a birthday gift from my partner, I received an upgrade to an executive suite facing Michigan Avenue.

- I answered the knock on the door to receive a two-layer chocolate birthday cake from the hotel.

- On the first morning, I savored a continental breakfast of salmon and plump red raspberries and fresh orange juice served in front of a churning wind and rain scene over Lake Michigan.

- At Macy's, I relished a facial from Yves St. Laurent and a complimentary fragrance from Donna Karan's "Cashmere Mist" scent.

- During afternoon tea in front of the fountain, I listened to the harpist nearby and dropped a coin in the fountain, reminiscent of Trevi in Rome.

- Celebrating music of four country singers at the Apollo Theatre I listened to the "Million Dollar Quartet," musical.

- On the second morning, I relished a full breakfast as I looked over the mounds of waves at the Lake on a sunny day

- Shopping at Filene's Basement, I manifested, by desire, a fuchsia ruffled cashmere sweater; albeit pink rather than lavender, I adapted.

- At noon, my mind cleansed by hearing the piano concert, by a Russian pianist playing Liszt and Schumann in the Fourth Presbyterian Church on the Magnificent Mile after church.

- Across the street, one of Chicago's finest Indian restaurants provided the setting for an exotic feast to close my two-day immersion.

ॐ

Celebrating the holidays with family in Chicago

My late cousin friend, Margot and I, performing at great grandmother's house in Chicago-land at Christmas.

My cousin was a highly regarded teacher who questioned all programs: "But are they learning?" She accomplished her desires of motherhood and a career while having multiple sclerosis.

Prayer in Celebration of Wholeness

Today in the quiet of the thick-stoned Fourth Presbyterian Church where our original families worshipped, I disappeared into the exquisite refinement and miraculous music played by a Russian pianist. My thought was, "God, how could I ever be as accomplished?" I felt body-washed by the God-in-man.

Sitting behind me and to the side was a cadre of African-Americans. On the steps coming in were several more "step" residents. They greeted me. The woman near me read her Bible throughout and after the concert. A cadre of four men behind her continued to sleep. At a soul level they had been nurtured by the music. We were alive. Thank you God, for life.

Seeing what is tangible and intangible—"the truth of the hour" assures me of "True North" for my life's course while I move along. I am aware of my wisdom after being fully present in the quiet of the desert at the Olgas. I can have faith to hold for the unknown beyond the stars as the sermon in the Outback proclaimed. I have equipped myself for the creativity which comes from wholeness because I trust my beliefs as a "Mantle of Safety."

APPENDIX

Find Your Spirit

We continue to migrate. I see that much of my expression in the world toward others has come from the heart of my ancestors "visiting upon the children." It has not been conscious imitating but rather the love of God bestowing through me to people who need it. Although I have not founded institutions to carry out the work in society, into the present and future, I wish I could and I am frustrated because I seem limited. But it is not my calling.

Hearing "my own sound" may migrate me even farther away from what is needed for others' good. Maybe what is needed for my good will picture and will expand in ripples. Otherwise, I do not know how to perpetuate the good of my sound or expand on it. Maybe I am like the incessant sound of the train announcing itself. I do pray the OT Jabez Prayer as an affirmation: "God, you bless me today. You expand my territory. Your hand is upon me. You keep me from evil."

I proclaimed a destiny for my beautiful Victorian house which seemed to everyone, totally destroyed by the mudslide. It lives through repurchase and restoration. What I acted out in refurbishing has been expanded. My migration lives on in spirit!

Where have I been? Where am I going?

I hear train whistles day and night from alongside the tracks near the Apple Shed.

I am reminded to make myself heard at each life crossing.

FOLKLORE OF MIGRATION STORIES

Literal migration stories are a family folklore story-type included in *A Celebration of American Family Folklore* by Zeitlin and Kotkin. Writing anecdotes in brief form preserves traditions. If one has told the stories, they are part of a story repertoire. According to Alan Dundes, they contain "folk idea"—belief and value content. The recall and writing will help show where one has been and where one is going.

The process I went through in artful living to restore my soul and creative life, to see my artistic self, is also possible for you. The artistry leads you to your soul and is, therefore, healing to wrong directions, weak career choices, addictions to cover pain, poor relations and loss of love. It is a deeper process than merely charting your flight migration.

However, the migration stories you have can lead you into more stories of your life and more awareness—a solid base from which "to fly." The stories from this book can be prompts and illustrations for you. It is my intention that they serve you as models while you take your own flight beyond the stars, through the unknown.

CREATE YOUR FLIGHT

Excerpted from *Dancing up the Mountain,*
A Guide to Writing Your Life Story,
Jacqueline K. Kelsey, PhD, 1999

"Where Have You Been?"
"Where Are You Going?"

I. How Many places have I lived?

Write the name places and dates on the blanks

1. _____
2. _____
3. _____
4. _____
5. _____

A. What is the relationship of the places to each other? Are they near/
far, low/high, in a circle, a spiral, a zigzag?

Briefly describe:

_____

_____

_____

B. Your picture: (Draw a diagram of the places in relationship to each
other.)

II. Choose a significant place change from _____ to _____

A. Why did you leave? Did it have a dramatic start?

Notes

_____

_____

_____

What is your Story?

B. *Was it a new beginning for the family or you? Do you tell this as part of your story? Where is the rest of your family now?*

Notes

_____

_____

_____

C. *Write your story on a 5x8 lined index card*

☑ *1. Make up a title and center it on the top line between quotation marks.*

☑ *2. On the left at the top of the card, write "Migration"*

☑ *3. On the bottom under the story, write Name, Place, and Date of your writing. Leave a bottom margin.*

☑ *4. Write only on the front side of the card. Save the back side of the card for extra notes.*

III. *How is your new beginning connected to their lives, moves, non-moves?*

A. *Are family connections part of your story?*

Notes

_____

_____

_____

Write your story on a 5x8 index card and label.

B. *Check the following details of <u>your</u> story:*

☐ *1. How did you go from one place to another?*

☐ *2. Who went with you? Were you alone and why?*

☐ *3. Was the place you chose important? Unimportant?*

☐ *4. Do you recall and identify with an ancestor(s) who migrated?*

Notes

_____

_____

_____

Are these details part of the story you tell? If not,
include them as additions on the back of the card.

Write your story on a 5x8 index card

C. *What were the struggles in the move?*
   Which struggles are part of the story you tell?
   Include these stories in your written migration story.

Notes

_____

_____

_____

Write your story on a 5x8 card.
Follow the directions for labeling under "B."

D. *What adjustments did you make to the new place? Are they funny*
   or sad, frustrating? Is this part of your "told" story?

   Notes

   _____

   _____

   _____

Write your story on a 5x8 card.

E. *Is your migration story part of a vision quest or a pilgrimage?*

   Notes

   _____

   _____

   _____

Write your story on a 5x8 card.

Notes for the back of the 5x8 card.

   _____

   _____

   _____

IV. Does anyone else in the family tell a story which is a spin-off on your migration? Who? On what occasions?

  A. Ideas

  1. They joined you.
  2. They visited you.
  3. They objected to your move.
  4. They recall ancestral moves.

  Write your story on a 5x8 card.

  B. Notes for the back of your story

  _____

  _____

  _____

V. Create three migration story cards

  A. Your ancestors' migration
  1. You may have only one or two lines.
  2. If no story is preserved, substitute an important historical migration you identify with.

  B. Your original family's migration

  C. Your most recent migration

Write your stories on a 5x8 cards.

D. *Ideas to include on Notes for the back*
1. *Is a lost fortune story connected?*
2. *What is your character portrait in the story?*
   Hero, Survivor, Innocent, Rogue?

Notes: 1. Lost Fortune

_____

_____

_____

Notes: 2. Character portrait

_____

_____

_____

VI. *Where are you headed in life?*

A. *Non-moving stories...*
   ☆ 1. *You refused to budge.*
   ☆ 2. *You'll never move again.*
   ☆ 3. *You are stuck.*

B. *Dream Moves*
   ☆ 1. *When I retire, I'm going to...*
   ☆ 2. *Next winter, I will be in...*
   ☆ 3. *When I get rich...*
   ☆ 4. *I'd love to live in...*

C. Tell your stories on 5x8 story cards

*On the back: Include important additional ideas,
facts, values, beliefs which are not part of the story.*

Migration

"The Bribe"

When my father made a job change from Chicago to take over my grandfather's glove factory, he moved to southern Illinois to my mother's hometown. I remember his being gone during the week and coming home on weekends. He announced finding our new house and enticed me toward the move by telling me about our new neighbors, a girl and her black dog. I loved dogs but I already had one named Brownie who was my lifeline. Somehow the girl and dog affected my willingness to move. My sister hated the move because we had to leave when our house sold and she did not get to graduate with her eighth grade classmates. It was traumatic for everyone. My first grade teacher thought I was less than bright because I would not talk and she recommended that I be held back a year. Mother said that she would not allow it.

Jacqueline K. Kelsey

Wells River, VT

February 1, 1999

Brownie, my confidant and soul mate.

LIFE'S TRANSCENDENT MIGRATION

As told in H. Glassie's *Passing the Time in Balleymenone*, the Irish farmer burns peat from his bog fields in the hearth at the center of his home. When he joins family and friends to tell stories of the workday in the fields, he joins field, community, and home. Stories become prayers spiraling in the smoke to eternity and infinitude.

The "Alpiner" wood stove in our Vermont living room, a
center for shared story with friends and neighbors.

For twenty years after reading about storytelling around the
hearth, I have told and written my own and others' life stories. The
stories have served as the launching pad enabling me to fly in the
dark beyond the stars because I believe these stories are full of God
in my life: Thank you God. "This is my story, this is my song." Story
spiraling from my day through an available conduit to infinitude
creates soul peace and sounds like the silence I described in the
Olgas. I am connected to God with my life.

TO THE READER

Dear Reader–

Every day in life is a transport, an ecstasy, if lived with true self-expression, which in the end comes from God, your soul's home. The right kind of self-expression pre-supposes wholeness, the full living-out of life with awareness of your inner self and the ambience surrounding us. All of this leads to wholeness of personality and when in our dreams and desires we "fly beyond the stars," we are likely to reach the substance of God, i.e., real, complete happiness grounded in satisfaction with ourselves and with life which is the tangible expression of the substance of God.

AN APOLOGY

I have spiritual gifts which I can illustrate. Unable to teach you my gifts, I invite you to see yours clearly when you fly BEYOND THE STARS

Tea time on the river bank with my friends.

INTERVIEW WITH THE AUTHOR ABOUT *FLIGHT BEYOND THE STARS*

Q. Why did you write the book?

A. I had envisioned a three-part series of books, the third being *Flying from the Mountain Top*. I arrived at *Flight Beyond the Stars* when I realized that what I experienced in everyday life and in my beliefs combined an adventure to see God more clearly in my life. It completes a spiritual migration I started twenty years ago in midlife. It seems that I get to celebrate my seventieth birth year by sharing it with others.

Q. Of what value is it to a reader who does not believe in God?

A. At least a reader can see how everyday life content leads to intangible truths which transcend the literal. It should be an encouragement to live more fully and to see that doing so is part of a larger understanding.

Q. Your non-linear approach of narrative and individual stories is a difficult means to use in order to see your understanding. How can you help a non-linear reader?

A. Life is sometimes like a dog's hind leg. Or rather, I see it as a sphere. Seldom do we get from A to Z easily or in a prescribed way. I pick according to the importance of events which contain substance. Put together, they add up much as life allows us to add them up, cumulatively and layered.

Q. Do you have faith?

A. I am growing in trust of the process over time. I have faith that God is tangible substance. There is no way to go but up because we were created to aspire.

Q. Are you a Christian?

A. How can I not be if I grow in my awareness of God being in all?—of Christ being the human representation of Himself, in the world.

Q. Is manifesting the same as guidance from God?

A. For me it is. It is my inner soul, one with God, showing faith.

Q. Is it frightening to fly beyond the stars?

A. Yes. Because the unknown is unsettling and change is difficult. However, it happens over time as we aspire to see more, do more, be more, and reflect more.

Q. Do you consider yourself out-of-the-ordinary?

A. No. But I am adventurous, spiritual and creative.

Q. What is the value of your book?

A. To show how viewing life creatively and expressively drives through difficult life circumstances to heal and to develop the soul, to bring fulfillment and enjoyment of life.

ABOUT THE AUTHOR

Dr. Kelsey is an alternative learner and leads others to connect and receive from out of the way people in society. Her greatest teachers are humble people and animals The collective wisdom of sixteen folks with dementia taught her about her own worth during her major transition. She portrays composite characters in the CD *Listening in the Moment to Timeless Folks*.

After a full career of teaching literature and writing in college and high schools, she became a teacher educator at the university level. Her research prepared the way for abandoning traditional learning in order to sing out with abandon and let her voice follow its own flow. The toning led her to perceive the chorus with others in a worldview based on nature.

To give over to a new person meant giving up former values and learned behavior, as well dependencies, except for God. Seeking new sources and connections required freedom and insecurity, and being in the dark about outcome.

Her interdisciplinary doctoral treatise on a nature-based worldview freed her to fly in the dark, beyond the stars, to live creatively, to find her own creative expression, and to accept a faith that God is in her everyday world. Jacqueline realized her dream to connect with original peoples in Hawaii, the Northwest, and the South Pacific.

LIST OF CONTENTS BY STORIES

COMPANION BOOK TO *FLIGHT BEYOND THE STARS*

BENEATH THE TALL BLACK DOOR, 2011
FOUR SEASONS ON RIVER STREET

John and Kathryn draw animals near to learn about finding joy in grief, balancing overwork with leisure, saying "no" to negative influences, and having faith to heal and confirm intuitive leads for career changes. The learning comes from seven stories with seven different animals that come to her front porch in the Northwoods.

Story events transform into everyday miracles which guide the characters' lives as well as the readers'.

Jacqueline shows how true events from her life reflect alternative living and learning. She is able to encourage others because of her own creative life.

Her professional research on imagination and nature provides her a philosophical basis for teaching, and also, provides inspiration for herself and other sojourners.

www.jacquelinekelsey70.com

BENEATH THE TALL BLACK DOOR, 2011
FOUR SEASONS ON RIVER STREET

CONTACT INFORMATION

Request radio and television appearances
as well as inspirational conference speaking:
please e-mail appleshed70@gmail.com.

Jacqueline invites your requests for phone conferencing
on writing and observing your story. 802-279-9825

Read and hear more about the author's other publications, life,
and writing at
www.jacquelinekelsey70.com.

This story about a humble wee mouse illustrates my perceptions of nature, flowers, and wildlife as one basis for my natural worldview — the basis of storytelling, writings and recordings at the Apple Shed. "Apple Mouse" is a mascot of the place and its creativity.

Part 1: Apple Mouse, The Gift Giver

Part 2: The Soul and Power of Place

A PLUMB LINE THROUGH LAYERS

Beginning with writing animal stories in the Northeast Woods, Jacqueline connects with early childhood caring for stray animals from the school playground, modeling her father's and grandmother's healing injured animals.

Her connection to the land comes from story and experience of the family farm in Pleasant Valley, northern Illinois, where her grandfather Kelsey farmed with his family and the King farm which her mother knew from childhood. Jacqueline's family played in the fields and woods of Gateway Farm, named by her grandmother Andrews for her and her husband's dairy farm, built up from the pioneer Blanchard family's estate of the 1820's.

Building up the *Apple Shed,* to house her creative nature writing and recording, is Jacqueline's expression of love for the land and plants and animals.

"Open my eyes that I may see. . ." - an old hymn

Printed in the United States
by Baker & Taylor Publisher Services